THE ACHILLES HEEL

by the same author

THE BURNED BRAMBLE
THE ABYSS
JOURNEY'S END

THE
ACHILLES HEEL

Manès Sperber

TRANSLATED BY
Constantine FitzGibbon

DOUBLEDAY & COMPANY, INC.
GARDEN CITY, NEW YORK, 1960

Contents

Introduction

'Achilles was not a true warrior, let alone a hero. The fact that he could hardly be wounded at all made it impossible for him to show what is normally known as courage. He therefore had no right to take part in men's battles.'

'A bad answer! Nought!' said the teacher. 'I have often noticed that it is almost impossible for Protestants or Jews to understand Greek mythology. They read the Bible too much. This has a lasting ill-effect on their minds.'

He let his eyes rest on Achilles' despiser. This was a poorly dressed, ill-nourished boy—a victim of the food shortages and the black market—who at the age of eleven was already clearly becoming enthralled by subversive ideas. The boy gazed back, an expression of melancholy pride in his eyes, and the schoolmaster, sensing in that gaze a criticism that made him feel uncomfortable, took refuge as usual in a minute act of self-love; he stroked his blond beard.

One year later, the winter of 1917—Vienna, a starving capital trembling with cold, was now the death chamber of the Austro-Hungarian Empire—the teacher asked: 'What do you know about the Gordian knot?'

'It was a knot that nobody knew how to untie, and Alexander the Great was no more successful than any of the others. Instead of accepting this fact, he cut the knot with his sword. Any halfwit could have done as much, if he'd had the guts. Alexander, with his armies behind him, knew that he was risking nothing. That is why his flatterers pretended to see an act of genius in what was simply the deed of a spoilt child.'

'And they were right.'

'No, sir, violence is not intelligence, and the cunning of black marketeers has nothing to do with genius.'

The teacher, too, hated those war profiteers who were starving him and his family. The faces of his children, like that of the boy

7

who had just spoken, resembled cubist portraits more and more each day. All the same he said: 'You start by exposing Achilles, you go on to debunk Alexander, and you will surely end up by attacking our dynasty and the foundations of our society. Is everything to be destroyed, as is happening at the present time in Russia? Is nothing still sacred to you?'

'Yes, sir, truth.'

'And what do you know about truth?'

'I know that it resembles no sort of lie.'

This was a generation, born with the century, which was to pick its way through the ruins of a civilisation that it had watched collapse in a welter of blood. For other generations truth had been a comfortable inheritance; in the eyes of this rebellious schoolboy and of many others like him, truth was a hostage which had to be snatched, violently, from the hands of the enemy. In order to conquer that enemy it was necessary to destroy all the sacred lies. This was why it was essential that Achilles be assigned to his proper place among the divine tricksters, that Alexander and all the conquerors be exiled from the Pantheon. This was why it was equally essential to despise any newspaper which had not been the victim of the censors, to condemn those writers and journalists who encouraged others to kill and die, while themselves taking good care to escape by glorifying that heroism to which they would condemn their contemporaries. Like their fellows on the opposite side, they pretended to defend civilisation whereas in fact all they were doing was dig its grave. Certainly they paid great attention to their style: they used their talents to depict countrysides torn asunder by shell fire, and to their fine phrases the innocent went to their death. A horrible beauty! A beauty harder to endure than hunger, cold, or the expression in the eyes of cripples.

We attended meetings held in bleak rooms normally reserved for the wedding parties or other social functions of the poor. The speakers, who usually belonged to some obscure socialist splinter group, demanded that the war be brought to an immediate end.

They spoke breathlessly: the police officer, seated beside the president of the meeting, could interrupt at any moment and forbid the speaker to go on, or even order the hall cleared. And these speakers had so much to say in order to proclaim the truth which the newspapers, working for the official propaganda, deformed with an apparently inexhaustible energy.

Outside the hall were the darkened streets, where the cold rain fell, and the representatives of law and order waited ready to pounce on those who had attended the meeting. The immediate answer was to sing the Internationale, and the song of the revolutionaries of 1905: 'Brothers, towards the sun, onward to liberty!' and the shouting of slogans. It was the boy's habit then to lead back the blind, consumptive ex-soldier, wounded in the war, to the distant suburb where he had managed to procure a bed but no place to stay during the daytime. (The dead alone were considered heroes in those days.)

During the long walk home, after he had said goodnight to the blind man, this precocious and solitary boy felt growing within him a tenderness, compounded of pity and of wonder, for this city, for its sleeping inhabitants, for these houses with their peeling, shabby paintwork, for the pavingstones that glistened beneath the endless autumn rains.

The clatter of his wooden shoes beat time to his unspoken thoughts: 'I hear your smothered breathing. I hear your heavy heartbeats, city of the sad!' He cut himself short, for he would not permit himself to use such words. He wished to banish all sentimentality, all those phrases which served to disguise the truth. The purpose of speech, he had decided, was simply to liberate ideas from that which conceals them, and to display existence in its nakedness. What mattered was the here and now, nothing else: the here and now, which must be freed from the immense weight of the past, and allowed to become the future. Yes, and this could happen at once, if only all those sleepers so desired it. Salvation is for today, salvation or disaster. The sailors of Kronstadt, the workers in the Putilov factories at Petrograd, were even now proving just this.

'So it is you, my eyes didn't deceive me! I remember the day when you condemned Achilles! Well, the Empire no longer exists and you should be overjoyed. But let us forget present misfortunes and speak of Achilles. He wasn't a true warrior and gave no proof of real courage, you used to say, because of his invulnerability. That's right, isn't it? Well, the Ulysses' and the Menelaus' are enjoying their old age, but Achilles died young, in battle. What have you got to say to that?'

'I am no longer interested in Achilles. They've just killed Kurt Eisner and Gustav Landauer, who were good and true men. In Munich the counter-revolution has begun . . .'

'You haven't answered my question', the schoolmaster insisted.

'It is only right and proper that Achilles and Siegfried and all their like should die young. If at long last the earth is to belong to men, then the gods and their bastards must be exiled from it once and for all. Every miracle is a crime, for miracles prevent men from acting, and transform our world into a great waiting room.'

'I do not care for people who take refuge in blasphemy when they run out of arguments. You have not answered my question.'

'I shall try to find an answer in the future.'

'So you admit that you do not know what that answer is?'

'Correct, but we shall find it.'

The young learned to question everything. But they were convinced that the most intractable problems would yield their solution to the courage and lucidity of those who desired nothing for themselves and everything for all the world: those for whom poverty was not the bitterly regretted absence of wealth, but the only form of liberation capable of annihilating that *Verdinglichung* of which Marx had spoken, that reduction to the status of, and hence domination by, things. Men were to be freed from the humiliating domination of things. This generation was constantly encountering the most audacious truths and discovering the answers to questions which it believed had never before been asked.

Revolutionary thought, obsessed by a future which it proclaims and whose conformation it awaits, returns ceaselessly towards the past and searches for heralds and prophets in forgotten tombs. Thus in the conquered countries after 1919 the young people began to dig deep into history. They read Marx and his disciples, but they devoured *The Decline of the West* even though they claimed to despise those currents of thought which emanated from Spengler. They smiled at Nietzsche's ignorance of sociology and at his political simplicity, but it was from his philosophy far more than from historical materialism that they derived one of their most cherished convictions: all the criteria and all the morality handed down from past generations must be scrapped once and for all. The young were determined to analyse, that is to say to take to bits, all those values which had been arranged hierarchically and to eliminate those of them which now were no longer anything except idols. We accepted Nietzsche's statement that Socrates was nothing but a particularly garrulous sophist, but all the same we continued to venerate that philosopher who had taught men how to die. Plato had pretended to despise poets, yet what we asked of him was not epistemology or political theory but poetic vision. We felt a great solidarity with Spartacus, Francis of Assisi, Spinoza, Saint-Just, Rosa Luxemburg, and in our breasts the young Russian terrorists of the nineteenth century kindled the same sentiments as did Rembrandt, Van Gogh, Cézanne and all the other artists neglected or unknown in their lifetimes.

We believed that we were the first generation to live consciously in a three-dimensional time; all the ages were ours, and since we ourselves belonged more to the future than to the present, we regarded ourselves as the brothers and contemporaries of those who had gone before. Disciples of Sigmund Freud or of Alfred Adler, we listened to what they taught as though their words were but the spoken echo of our own intuition.

The word 'becoming' was our favourite. It seemed to imply everything—that to be is often tragic, and that to pretend to be is always comic. We would not admit that mysteries existed, and we distrusted those who claimed that they did. For a man aware of his own ignorance and who seeks for no proud pretexts to defend that ignorance, what is unknown is neither more nor less mysterious than darkness. Darkness does not deprive objects of their place, form or colour; it simply decreases their visibility.

A man walking across a desert is suddenly confronted by a lion. He puts his umbrella to his shoulder, shouts: 'Bang! Bang!' and the wild beast falls dead. A mystery? Not at all. Behind the man with the umbrella, although he did not know this, was standing a hunter with a loaded rifle. Dismiss the man with the umbrella crying: 'Bang! Bang!', and the event, now inserted in a perfectly satisfactory causality, remains unchanged. Alas, the majority of our masters were 'bang bangers'! Our thirst to know everything was itself a drunkeness. We searched everywhere—in psychology and in Marxism, in the biblical prophets, in Shakespeare, Dostoievsky and Nietzsche, everywhere we were looking for the same quality: lucid passion. Was passion to show us the ends of our own action, and was lucidity to guide us towards those ends, or were their rôles reversed? We did not ask this question, for everything presented itself to us in the form of a dialectical unity. The antithesis was born with the thesis and together they faded away into the synthesis which itself became the new thesis. Everything was in movement, and movement was all.

But our time was rationed and the last phase was drawing nigh. Preparations must be made without delay: the strategy and tactics of revolution had to be learned, as well as the psychology of abandoned children: psychical methods of standing up to torture, as well as the fundamental principles for a post-revolutionary aesthetic which would make it impossible for a Van Gogh to die miserably through lack of recognition. Arrangements must be made to avoid the risk of corruption by power, and to elaborate scientifically the rules for a hygiene of the spirit as effective as the hygiene of the body. Lies must be expunged from the history books, and their true countenance given back to all those whom the conquerors had disfigured or condemned to oblivion. There was so much to do . . .

To begin with, the men of yesterday had to be defeated. Those journalists and writers, for example, who had remained faithful supporters of the monarchy, expansionists and the chanticleers of

war, had not been driven down into the valley of silence but on
the contrary, on the very morrow of the revolution, had been
installed in comfortable situations from which the republic had
lacked the courage to expel them. And everybody seemed to have
forgotten the past which was yet so close.

We lacked hatred. Having learned that the master is himself the
victim of the system on which his domination is based, we envied
him neither his wealth nor his power. We were going to abolish
both wealth and power for ever. But for the public figures of
society, for its figureheads and spokesmen, we felt a limitless
contempt. Their opportunism which made them approve of all
that could favour their own interests, their vanity, finally their
cowardice, this all transformed antagonists whom we would have
had tragic into squalid little figures in a comedy played by persons
who did not know how to act. And these amateurs constantly
missed their cues, answering too soon or too late, or falling over
one another in their anxiety to get onto, or off, the stage.

The affair of the Gobelin Tapestries was one episode in this
comedy. The Empire had lost the war, and the Austrian Republic
had emerged from it as from a shipwreck. One third of the
inhabitants of the new state lived in Vienna, where they continued
to starve to death; each day produced its new quota of dead
children or adolescents, killed by consumption, in the families of
the working class. The misery in which the masses lived was
assuming terrifying proportions. An American Corporation
offered to feed the city in exchange for those Gobelin tapestries
which had formerly belonged to the Emperor. The Austrian
reaction was furious and immediate: 'We would sooner die of
hunger than part with our heritage! Anything rather than lose
the Gobelins!'

Apart from certain specialists and a handful of enthusiasts,
nobody had ever shown the slightest interest in these particular
Gobelins. Those 'representatives of Austrian culture' who now
set themselves up as the tapestries' most zealous and violent
protectors, had never previously taken the trouble even to go and
look at them. These 'souls', encased in well-fed bodies, derived
an extreme satisfaction in this struggle for decorative objects

which in fact meant very little to them. But by protecting these
'artistic treasures' inherited from the Empire, they thought to
prove their right to act, and be regarded, as an élite. The whole
affair was an <u>amalgam</u> of fictional values and grotesque publicity,
save of course the misery of the people, willingly forgotten and
insulted by these aesthetes who for four years had praised the
infinite beauties of mechanised carnage, and by those moralists
who had not hesitated to justify the worst crimes committed by
the men in power.

This episode, quite unimportant so far as its material results
went, was yet heavy with significance. Many young men had
hesitated before entering any political party, held back by
scruples concerning intellectual honesty: now they felt that they
no longer had any right to remain outside the revolutionary
movement. In fact they drew the obvious conclusions from the
existing condition of affairs, an action that right wing anti-
communists have never been able to understand. Even today such
people cannot conceive that certain sequences in a Russian
film—*The Battleship Potemkin*—should have pushed young
intellectuals to abandon their careers and to become professional
revolutionaries. Heavily booted feet clattering down a wide stair-
way: a baby's pram, abandoned by the child's mother who has
been shot down, rolling towards the edge of the abyss: a legless
cripple attempting desperately to crawl away from the rifles of
the Czar's soldiers that are pointing towards him . . . Wherein lies
the power of these images? In many cases their effect was far
greater than that of Lenin's best writings.

We thought to have banished all sentimentality from our
hearts. We forbade ourselves to be good. But the picture of that
baby carriage, of that legless cripple pursued by the heavy boots,
created within us an emotion so intense that it was only tolerable
when transformed into energy. We did not have to look for
reasons to rebel; they were all about us; our awareness of
contemporaneity discovered these reasons thanks to a 'while'
motive, an obsessive motive deriving from a sentimental education
which will probably end only with our death.

'While we as tourists were exploring and admiring the narrow lanes of Florence, our fellows in Mussolini's gaols in the Lipari Islands were despairing of our solidarity ... While we stood lost in thought before Titian's pictures, the inhabitants of Venice were sinking ever deeper into hopeless misery ... While we in the first tender light of dawn were setting out to climb a high mountain, the miners were resignedly going down into the bowels of the earth ...'

This awareness of contemporaneity and these juxtapositions extracted from every experience the same inevitable lesson: society must be changed. And at once! Patience became a crime when confronted by ['the categorical imperative of overthrowing all those conditions in which man exists as a humiliated, enslaved, abandoned and contemptible being] (Marx).

'How to become that which one is?' This was the question put by Nietzsche when searching for what was best in himself. How to arrange that man shall become that which he is to himself: the supreme being? We hunted for the answer as if we were thus preparing to establish the preliminary conditions for one immense insurrection, of which the victory would be not an ending but a beginning. We shall never be, we shall always be becoming, 'and the centuries shall not efface the mark of our passage across this earth', we said, quoting Schiller: for we intended to put an end to pre-history.

We did not wish to be heroes. Everything in traditional heroism revolted us: the grandiloquence of acts as much as that of words and gestures. Psychology had rendered boldness suspect in our eyes; we thought that we would know how to be brave when the necessity arose, but we aimed at a courage which permits the avowal of fear and its conquest. We examined the pinched faces of our fellows who had escaped from those countries where the White Terror was in action, and we asked ourselves whether we would have the strength to resist torture. Would we prefer death or dishonour?

For we had silently re-established the concept of honour—an honour which curiously resembled that of Don Quixote. We had also, again silently, established a morality which was unusually strict. We only had one word with which to express it—solidarity.

In consequence we felt the need to free ourselves from every form of pose, to abandon all artifice and all those forms which support insincerity, always to remain close to the true source and to value only 'man in his nakedness': to find the most direct form of speech, stripped of all phraseology and any seductive ornamentation, not in order to simplify complex facts, but to make the essence of those facts accessible to all. 'Let thy yea be yea, thy nay be nay': this was a simplification which we had to guard against. Light for us only existed when it had been taken by force from darkness conquered. And we only believed in our own strength in the measure that we had created it by surmounting and transforming our own weaknesses.

For we knew that we were vulnerable at all times, even though we served an Achilles, that invincible proletariat to whom history had promised the inevitable and final victory.

'Show me any illusion that I still cherish, and I shall root it out at once,' thus spoke the young man who at the age of eleven had begun his fight against all myths. He and his like were aware that the postwar epoch was only a precarious armistice, the antecedent to a second world war which nobody desired and for which everyone was already making preparations; that a crisis of exceptional gravity would soon shake the very foundations of capitalism throughout the world, and that in consequence revolution and counter-revolution would find themselves face to face with immensely strong forces at the disposal of each; that misery would throw the masses into the political arena, and that for the first time politics would really become the destiny of each and every human being.

They were without illusions, or so they thought, but not without hope: they were prepared to go through a period of catastrophe which they accepted in advance. And later? The exits from purgatory could only lead to paradise. Until then it was not a question of pitying the unhappy nor even of helping the afflicted, but of making use both of the one and of the other. It was not goodness that was needed but efficiency: efficiency in the service of a future good. They quoted the case of Felix Dzerzinski, a Russian revolutionary of Polish origin, to whom Lenin had given the terrifying job of running the Cheka, because, as was said, he was a pure man with no taste for violence.

'All those who have hitherto made use of violence have ended by becoming its slaves. But we, we shall be its masters, because even while we are making use of it we shall know that it is contemptible.' Thus spoke the young man while addressing a public meeting organised as a protest against the injustice hanging over the heads of Sacco and Vanzetti, the innocent anarchists.

All that he said, both then and later, about the faults of others was true; what he said about his own people and about their sort of violence began as an illusion, developed into a mistake, and finally flourished as a lie. In order to defer awareness of this, he had to conjugate his verbs more and more in the future tense, the old and well-tried trick of all imposters; 'Kill and die in order that your children may live in eternal peace'; 'Suffer yourselves in order that your grandchildren shall never know misfortune'; 'Jam tomorrow!'

Truth is that which resembles no sort of lie—thus had the child already made his passionate affirmation. The young man, tormented by doubt, tried to find consolation in another formula: 'Our truth shall finally cease to resemble a lie, if only we can manage to remain unconditionally faithful to it.'

'Forgive me for calling on you at such a very early hour. Perhaps you do not recognise me? I am an old man these days and you too have grey hair ... I read your name in the papers published by the occupying powers. You're on the side of the conquerors now. This may well lead you to believe that you were right in the old days, that you are still right today ... Do you not recognise me?'

The date was early in the winter of 1946, the place the capital of the second Austrian Republic, now cut into four small portions.

'I am delighted to see you again, professor. Won't you sit down?'

'On the one hand one might say that nothing whatever has changed. Hunger is back again, there is no coal to heat our freezing houses, the black market is with us. And the Americans, the English and the French are once again numbered amongst our conquerors, exactly as happened thirty years ago. But on the other hand it cannot be denied that everything is quite different. Why? Because there are no longer any rebels of your sort. Vanished into thin air! The real European rebellion is *kaput*! You thought yourselves to be the first generation which ... who ... in all matters ... As a matter of fact what you were was the last rebellious generation. You were not the advance guard but, so to speak ... a placenta. When you opened the door to me you thought that I had come to beg for cigarettes, didn't you? And I may say I would accept some with gratitude. But what is even more important to me than cigarettes is to be done with your arrogance—the arrogance that was yours thirty years ago. I would like to know if you have at long last finally uncovered the true significance of the myth of Achilles.'

'Please take as many cigarettes as you wish, but tell me yourself what it is that I should have discovered. In the old days you never asked questions without first being quite certain that you yourself knew the answers.'

'Fair enough! I affirm that the cause which you espoused had been declared inevitably victorious. So you entered the struggle with certitudes far more consoling to yourselves than those which supported Achilles when he defied Hector. Far more consoling, for you lacked even a vulnerable heel. You agreed to do battle in conditions which made you a super-Achilles, not as individuals but as a cause, a cause with a capital C!'

'Your parallel does not convince me, for we were men struggling against men and ...'

'It is presumably precisely for that reason that the cause has become dehumanised ... I have never been to Russia, but Russia has come to us. We know her now for what she is, her revolutionary army and her police, the flaming sword of the revolution. The workers of Floridsdorf, of Brigittenau and of all the other working class quarters can tell you what they have learned since they have established contact with proletarian power.'

'That is well known.'

'What do you mean: 'that is well known'? Did you ever talk about it? Where? What were your protests?'

'And how about yourself, professor, when confronted by the Nazis and their crimes?'

'For myself, I have never been a revolutionary nor even a reformer. When the republic replaced the monarchy I submitted without protest, as you know. Whatever the régime may be, I obey its laws; I neither make them nor discuss them. As Socrates, unjustly condemned to death . . .'

'So you were an accomplice of Hitler's . . .'

'Nonsense! In 1938 I retired on a pension. In 1940 I was compelled to take up schoolmastering again. My son set off for the war. He will never come back. When the porter came and told me to fly the swastika flag, I obeyed. Nowadays when the self-styled delegate of the District Commission suggests that I put out flags, I still obey. I fly two blood-red flags from the window of our diningroom. The apartment of my wife's great-grandfather, in which we have lived since we were married, is in the second district; therefore our colour is red, with hammers and sickles scattered here and there . . . Hitler's accomplice yesterday, Stalin's today? You're mad if you cannot see the disproportion between those personalities and myself. What is more, you seem to have forgotten that I am a monarchist. I think, as I have always done, that nothing can satisfactorily replace an old dynasty which no longer needs to affirm its legitimacy. That is all . . .'

'Then how about the Rosenbaums, that old couple who lived across the landing from you with their grand-daughter? They were insulted before being taken off to the slaughterhouse. What did you do to help them, to save them?'

'Nothing, obviously. During the years of which you speak I was busy revising my doctoral thesis on: "The use of the adverbs *haud* and *haudquaquam* in Latin prose and verse". But let us turn to yourself. Tell me the names of those innocent people whom you have saved. How many of them are there? A hundred? Not so many? Fifty? Ten? No? Five . . . not even five? Only one—yourself? So you have not saved a single innocent being! No, I failed to save the Rosenbaums, that's true. My duty has always seemed to me a modest and extremely limited one. But what about you and your fellows? I saw you setting off early one

morning astride the horses of the apocalypse, riding towards the
skies to clear them for ever of the gods and of God Himself! Now
you are back, you have driven your horses to death, but the skies
are still not empty. You transformed them into billets for the
Hitlers, the Stalins, *e tutti quanti.* Is that what you wished to do?'

'No.'

'Which means that you have failed miserably, even though
today you find yourselves in the camp of the victors.'

'Yes.'

'And you are clearly aware that yours is not the first generation
to have suffered a similar misfortune. Your cause, like Achilles, is
dying because it has been wounded in the lowest part of its
anatomy,' the schoolmaster ended with an expression of triumph.

He listened politely but without apparent interest while his
former pupil tried to show him that just causes can even survive
their defeats; that though the struggle may be lost, this does not
mean that it has been senseless. 'We erred in our choise of means,
we took the wrong road, but as for our objective . . .'

The old man politely hid his impatience while awaiting the end
of a discourse which he appeared to know by heart already.

'Professor, you have doubtless heard of greyhound races. The
electric hare is always faster than the dogs, and finally disappears
behind a wall against which the dogs bang their muzzles. I wrote
somewhere or other: "If one dog should finally succeed in
catching this hare what would he learn? That he has spent his
whole life chasing a tin object which will give him an electric
shock the moment he touches it". And I added: "If I were that
dog, I should do all in my power to catch the electric hare, even if
I knew it for what it was".'

POSITIONS
An Essay on the Left

Extracts from this essay were published in numbers 26 and 27 of the review *Preuves* (April and May 1953) with the title *Ideology and Society.*

Positions — An Essay on the Left

There is a rumour current in the world. Lost in a fog of foolish confusions, exhausted by useless efforts, the left died yesterday or the day before. And those who spread this rumour add that the terms 'left' and 'right' are henceforth void of all meaning.

It is both ridiculous and sad to deny one's own death, and to demand a reprieve of gravediggers anxious to finish their job quickly. But we are still alive, and we can see quite clearly, so far as we are concerned, what is ours and what is not. Certainly the left is threatened by bad victories and misunderstood defeats. Nevertheless, even though condemned to death, the left cannot die save by suicide. And there are many of us who have no inclination to suicide, and who will not seek refuge in that consoling bitterness which nourishes the manias of the apocalypse and the voluptuous joys of despair.

Each generation suffers from the illusion that everything can be and should be decided in its lifetime: ours thought to see valid reasons for acting as though this eternal illusion was henceforth justified by fundamental truth. To live without certainties is possible, but to undertake and to carry through great designs is not.

In all ages the left has been engaged in a struggle against the absolute, which is the sublime mask of magical, religious or philosophic negations. The position of the left can be defined as the negation of a negation. It has been affirmed by those who have suffered and died on its behalf; the monuments to its victories are tombs, its flags are shrouds stained with blood, with its own blood and not with that of its enemies.

During the summer of 1914 the capitals of Europe were filled with joy, as though this were the preparation for a feast of universal brotherhood, an immense banquet such as that of which Danton had dreamed, an *agape* which would finally reconcile all men to their brothers. It was during this summer of 1914 that the left suffered its greatest defeat, a defeat from which it has never recovered. Like love, victory devours its own causes, while defeat redoubles those causes. The only escape lies in self-transformation, in release from that which deserves to be defeated.

In 1914 the left—that is to say the working class and its organisations as well as the intellectuals—identified itself with power: it embraced a cause which to it was masked: and it is for those masked ends that ten million Europeans died: innocents killing other innocents.

The ideologists announced that this was a left-wing war. The Germans marched against the Czar; had not Karl Marx demanded that Prussia, after conquering Louis Bonaparte, should finally settle with Russia, the policeman of Europe? Did not old August Bebel offer to set off himself, a rifle on his shoulder, against the oppressors of St Petersburg? The Allies marched against Germany and the Hapsburg Empire. And was not this a fine cause, the liquidation of Prussian militarism and the liberation of the peoples oppressed by Franz-Josef? After this war, the war to end wars, the whole world would embrace democracy, such was the proclamation of this positive left wing.

But a left wing reconciled to power is an irreconcilable contradiction in terms. We knew it, we who were very young in those days, and we turned to Communism because the names of Rosa Luxemburg, Lenin, Trotsky, Bukharin, Liebknecht, Ruehle, were the courage and the honour of the left. We knew that this handful of names had swung against the current. The new world which emerged so slowly from the deluge of blood seemed to us an abject thing. We had no wish to belong to it, and we desired no part in its victories. That is why we were so quickly convinced that the surrender by the left in 1914 had been due to treason on the part of the leaders of the workers' movement.

In accepting this explanation, the new left wing, which came into existence after the Russian Revolution and the end of the war, set off along a road that led straight into countless errors and misfortunes. And one of the most cardinal of these was the travesty of fundamental principles, the corruption of minds, the replacing of historical materialism by a police conception of history.

The destiny of the left in this century will be worked out in the struggle that it must fight against this new right wing. Meanwhile it must continue its battle against the old right wing which is always with us, and which does not attempt to disguise its nature beneath flags stolen from a murdered revolution. In order to know your enemy, it is essential first to know yourself.

I

'The dominant ideology is the ideology of the dominant class', so taught Marx. From one point of view this statement is self-evident, from another it contains an element of falsehood. The dominant class does not produce its own ideology: it is not that class which in the old days invented its divine origin and later its divine right, which established its ceremonial and so forth. It had to be taught all that, even as there are specialised servants employed in the mansions of noblemen who teach their masters how to appear noble. The creators of ideologies, the magicians, priests, artists or philosophers, do not belong to the dominant class. They are its slaves, its employees or its tradesmen, convinced that they are serving the establishment and the consolidation of a 'natural' order, eternal, desired by God, justified by reason, in conformity with human nature, evidently good, or perhaps evidently evil ... There is no example of a power group which has not found intellectuals ready to justify and glorify its reign, and to prove beyond argument that it is the logical and final conclusion to all that has gone before.

Thus the right, whether it be of revolutionary or other origin, is born whenever power arises. Justified and legitimised by the very fact that power exists, it then justifies and legitimises all that power is. The conception, development and death of the right is one long process of symbiosis. It is a mistake, which enjoys a fairly wide currency among the men of the left, to assume that those of the right are by definition opportunists. A true right wing ideologist can detest his king throughout his entire life; can withdraw into misery and disgrace while remaining a convinced royalist; for he regrets and even opposes those human accidents which royalty makes possible.

The dominant ideology is thus the product of ideologists working for the establishment. It always corresponds to a conception of the social order which has been adopted as essentially definitive.

By contrast the ideology of the left is originally defined in negative terms: it considers the existing order to be a mere disorder, protected and ill-concealed by the establishments of a power that is *a priori* condemned to die, as have died all those powers which have preceded it. Authoritarian power is an inhuman imposture deriving from violence and cunning: such is the fundamental principle of left wing ideology. 'It is quite impossible to reign innocently', said Saint-Just, referring to Louis XVI. But he himself, after a brief career of power, did not die the death of an innocent man.

The ideology of the left wishes to convince and not to dominate. It thus tends towards a society in which man shall not be governed but shall be master of his own liberty, and where the act of government shall be finally replaced by the administration of affairs. This ideal community would be created by the *consensus omnium*, the pooling and mutual acceptance of its citizens' inalienable liberties, while the society's institutions would be finally stripped of their sacred quality and would become simply means, tools. Indeed the left can be nothing except radical. This is explained as follows: 'A theory becomes acceptable to the masses when it is displayed *ad hominem*, and it is displayed *ad hominem* when it becomes radical. To be radical means to go to the root of everything. Now for man the root is man himself... A radical examination of religion leads to the doctrine that for man, man himself is the supreme being: and therefore to the categorical imperative of overthrowing all those conditions in which man exists as a humiliated, enslaved, abandoned and contemptible being...'

Thus did Karl Marx, at the age of twenty-five, express his criticism of Hegel's philosophy of law, two years after he had rejected his philosophy of the state. Hegel's philosophy of the state is perhaps epitomised in the following characteristic remarks taken from his *Philosophy of History:* 'The state does not exist for its citizens, but rather it might be said that it is their end and they are its tools . . . The divinity of the state is idea as it exists on earth.' Thus speaks the right.

That every man should be an end in himself, and should be a means to no other man, is what Kant had taught. In 1784, speaking of 'the enlightenment (*Aufklärung*) and of peace' he wrote: 'Enlightenment is man's abandonment of that immaturity for which he is himself responsible. Immaturity (youth) is the inability to make use of one's own understanding without letting oneself be directed by another. Man is responsible for this immaturity when it is not due to a lack of understanding but to a lack of resolution and of courage in making use of his understanding without outside direction. *Sapere aude!* Dare to make use of your own intelligence! That is the motto of the enlightenment.'

As can be seen, there is thus no possible field of agreement between the left and the right. The right recognises nothing save the established order and its authority, the left nothing save men. But let us avoid one error: if we accept only the laws of formal logic, then the system of the right alone can be achieved.

In such a system what is meant by individual liberty? Simply that fragment of power which the state delegates, or rather lends, to the individual. It exists only because the state, sole source and possessor of all powers, and therefore sole source of all liberties, wishes this, and for just so long as it wishes it. The individual is truly free, and feels himself to be so, when he identifies himself submissively with the state and loses himself in it as the part is lost in the whole. Only he who cuts himself off from the state does not feel free. He is abusing his rights, is a fraud, a secret enemy. For what is this liberty that the state's opponent demands? The liberty to think otherwise. Now only an enemy can feel the need for such liberty. He is therefore a purely negative, destructive force, the incarnation of crime. For what source of law or liberty can there be outside of the state, outside of the established power? Since man himself is not this source, the state's opponent is the representative of another power, the agent and lackey of that power. In order thus to deceive his benefactors (the state and its leaders), it is certain that the individual must be a pervert, a scoundrel. Only a scoundrel would describe as oppression or persecution what is merely the enlargement of the liberties of the state, of the establishment, of a church, a monarchy, etc. The part cannot be the whole, and a tool does not rebel. It becomes useless. Even before having been expelled from the whole, the part that has revolted has already ceased to exist.

The state is reason: therefore no man can hold up reason against it. It is incorruptible innocence, it is infallible. The man who is accused by the state is condemned in advance. The accused who would defend himself further proves by so doing that he is an enemy: he pretends that reason is on his side and against the state, he aspires to the criminal liberty of thinking otherwise. The refusal to confess, even to confess falsely, is in itself a crime.

This perfectly logical philosophical polity of the right has almost never been formulated in precise terms. From Plato to Hobbes and Hegel, the philosophers have approached such a polity without however completely becoming identified therewith. And in civilised communities its realisation has hitherto never been possible for obvious reasons: stresses within the ruling classes, the threat provided by the classes aspiring to power, the opposition between generations, the neighbourhood of other and less oppressive states, finally the weakness as well as the strength of human nature, all prevented the construction of this ideal state. We had to wait until our own time to see it become the reality. It claims that Marx and socialism inspired it, and it announces itself as the heir of all the traditions of the left.

'Instead of hoisting banners, those aristocrats donned the rags of proletarian beggars in order to persuade the people to follow them. But as soon as the people fell in at their heels, they saw upon the backs of their leaders the same old feudal coats-of-arms, and they scattered amidst mocking laughter.'

Here again Marx erred through optimism. At the present time

there exist intellectuals who describe themselves as being of the left because they fell in behind those banners at the very moment when, on the backs of their leaders, were revealed the coats-of-arms of Ivan the Terrible and of Peter the Great.

The pseudonymous nature and the faulty terminology implicit in the ideologies of the right derive from their pseudo-mania; this reflects the inevitable contradiction between the practice of power and the theory upon which it claims to be based. Such an ideology becomes in part abstract mythology, in another part a system of sanctified lies.

Any oligarchical régime, and all the more so any autocratic one, lives beneath the compulsion of falsifying its own history in order to invent a new origin for itself; it must kill its past and replace it by another which will prove that it is in fact the future, realised here and now. Playing all the major rôles, it must show that it is both its own father and its own son, that it is eternity condensed. The best means of killing its past is to make some of the witnesses to that past its accomplices and to liquidate all the others. Hegel was right: such a state is divine, its liberty unlimited, for it can affect the past; truth, like man, has merely become one of its tools, easily replaceable. The more power becomes absolute, the more everything that is not power becomes relative thereto. Power alone is now essential and therefore reasonable. It alone exists. Everything else exists, or does not exist, depending on that power.

As for the left, it has dreamed since first it existed of a final reconciliation between theory and practice. So long as these are not united, they remain separated by the lies which the ideologists invent, and linked to one another by the illusions from which the oppressed and the exploited draw their sustenance.

The left has always been materialistic, at least in the sense that it has refused to take ideologies into account, and that, pushing them aside like so many curtains, it has attempted to reveal to the eyes of the world the real social relationships, the concrete conditions in which men live. Every revolution begins with a denunciation of deeds and facts. 'Don't look at his lips, look at his fists!' said Martin Luther.

The left therefore believed in the virtue of truth, and that consciousness was critical insofar as it implied awareness both of itself and of society and history. And it needed to believe that nothing was final, that the future would resemble neither the past nor the present, and that movement in time would be inevitably upwards, a development, a continual progress.

Until the end of the eighteenth century the left expressed itself in ethical and logical terms which were relatively concrete, as did Spinoza for example. Since the French Revolution it has defined its position according to a philosophy of history which, a century ago, was due to spell the end of all philosophy and should have done away even with itself through self-realisation: once realised, it should have radically transformed a world that had already been so abundantly interpreted.

2

Let us envisage a theatrical performance of which no man knows why nor how it started. In the audience are seated a deaf man and one who is blind. From time to time the one and then the other drop off to sleep. When they awake they are first of all astonished to discover that all has changed while they slumbered, and then, after a few minutes, equally astonished to notice that in reality nothing has changed whatsoever. The actors' gestures, which only the deaf man can observe, are in shocking disharmony with the words that they accompany. But these are only audible to the blind man, and he has only the sketchiest knowledge of the language in which they are spoken, which is the language of his deaf companion.

Considerably later they attempt to tell a stranger the little that their defective memories have retained of this play that they failed to comprehend (and that may, who knows, be incomprehensible). This stranger then writes a coherent and logical account of what he has heard: such is History. In History's account everything has a meaning. There is no effect without its cause, no act without a previous intent: the past has become the infancy of the present, which itself is full maturity seen in the golden light of midday.

Following in the footsteps of so many others, Homer tells the story of the Trojan War, a history of crimes and of punishments. Why so many misfortunes? Because Helen, the heroine of some Offenbach operetta, has been abducted by an elegant young man? So much noise and anger for so little? Not at all, there is a story behind the history; three top-ranking goddesses had all picked on the idea of being elected Miss Olympus by this particular young man. When the goddesses quarrelled, the nations had to die.

So the human tragedy would merely be the epilogue to a divine comedy; to understand the history of men, it would be necessary to know the ins and outs of the scandals on Olympus. Life thus becomes a puppet theatre, in which the puppets are endowed with astonishing skills but lack the power to influence their own destinies. The reign of God is the reign of the past, of ancestral animals preserved in totemism and of ancestral spirits preserved in animism. It is true that the religions are greater than these magical elements, but they have integrated and not eliminated such relics within themselves. We know of societies that have invented their ancestors, but we know of none that has been able to live without any. In these facts from the past men seek to decipher the sense of the present, the promises and threats of the future. Destiny thus speaks an archaic tongue.

In our civilisation the great change was marked by the appearance of the prophets of Israel; the eschatology of an Isaiah foresees the end of history and its accomplishment in the final peace which all beings will conclude with God and with one another, when the present shall become eternity, an indestructible harmony. Paradise was offered to Adam and Eve in order that they live there, not that they act there; their first action resulted in their expulsion from Paradise. History begins when harmony is broken, and will end in a great metamorphosis. All the world will become Paradise, and the country of exile be transformed into the home-land; nothing will then separate the creature from his Creator. In the course of history—that long and hard apprenticeship which is yet a constant progress—men are learning to make the one final unity, which is humanity. Time, that drop thrown off by eternity, will be abolished, and human beings will regain the immortality promised to Adam and Eve before they had committed their act. The movement of history is therefore only a return journey by devious paths. Before the expulsion it sufficed to be created in order to last; afterwards it was necessary to merit such endurance by actions, and through them to reconquer the right to eternity. In creating humankind God embarked upon an experience by which He intended to shed a fragment of His infinitude and limit His omnipotence; He was giving to man the freedom of choice between justice and injustice, between the true and the false.

History is thus the story of a love between the Creator and his created, with episodes often both sad and cruel. It can culminate only in a happy union. But when? That depends on man. (In the religion of Zoroaster, an eschatology more or less contemporaneous with that of the Jews, it will all depend upon the outcome of the struggle between Ormuzd and Ahriman.)

The life of each generation therefore resembles an examination. If the generation passes that examination, the result is not only their own redemption but the redemption of all those beings that have ever lived before them. There is neither an afterlife nor a reincarnation; but resurrection is promised. Death will die, and the dead shall live.

This conception, based upon an implicit theodicy and on an ethic with clearly formulated postulates, has been in certain minor respects modified since Isaiah's time. Its main propositions can be summarized as follows:

1. Human history is a continual movement towards an end, and therefore a progress or ascent, though sometimes with vagaries which can lead mankind away from that end, with descent and even falls that for a certain time will hinder the upward climb, but these are unimportant *sub specie humanitatis*.
2. Becoming, being and disappearing, acting and suffering, are always reasonable because they are both determined and determinants. In general that which is is reasonable, and vice versa.

3. Knowledge of the reasons of history permits an acceleration of its rhythm by avoiding certain vagaries and certain descents; it also teaches man a better knowledge of himself, of his rôle as a human being on this earth, and makes of being a continual becoming.

4. The end of history is at hand, far closer at hand than the unaware suspect. It will happen in your time, even in your lifetime. (Therefore you must live as if it depended solely on yourself that the Messiah shall come tomorrow at first light, or that the revolution shall take place tomorrow afternoon, or at the latest early on the day after!)

Metaphysics is an a-historical discipline. Its two branches, ontology and epistemology, are but a search for the eternally human: the metaphysician is a philosopher who, in effect, has changed only slightly throughout the past few thousand years, looking always for knowledge and usually finding only terminologies. The labours of Penelope, that sly and faithful wife, were, as we know, remarkably unproductive. They did not serve to clothe the naked, and even she herself needed the work of slaves to provide her dresses.

Greek philosophy elaborated a cosmology and a metaphysical system, but no conception of history. Thucydides at his most optimistic hoped that the experience of his own age would be useful to future generations in teaching them how to avoid the errors of the past—useless wars and crimes, and those atrocious deeds which, scattered like seed, bring forth a harvest of hatred. He was close to Socrates without ever naming him (and the Socrates to whom he does refer is not the philosopher). Plato's master taught: 'Men can, and therefore must, learn to be virtuous.' He was the first to look for a system in which there would be a place for man both as subject and object, a system which would finally no longer have room for the usurping gods. He was the first person in the non-Jewish world to wish to subordinate established institutions to the individual's conscience. In Plato's political adventures we see reflected his conviction that history could assume a sense, on condition that it became a field of action for philosophers. His experiments in Syracuse were intended to prove not that history is reasonable nor that it has a meaning, but that it is rationalisable once it becomes a lived philosophy beneath the rule of a virtuous élite invested with all powers. (And it may be remarked that throughout his life Plato remained faithful to the ideas, and even more so to the political ambitions, of his youth—although he gave them a new expression.)

Victorious Christianity abolished metaphysics and imposed a philosophy which Saint Augustine explained clearly in his *City of God,* when he proclaimed that history has already found its end in the final collapse of the Roman Empire. From the creation of the world until the coming of the Saviour, all had been determined by providence. In the ensuing centuries the attempt was made to eliminate all that derived from Paganism, for there could be nothing true save biblical history as interpreted in the Christological sense. For a thousand years minds were obsessed by a philosophy which inspired them with a feeling that they were struggling in a post-historic period, in an antichamber to Hell or to Heaven. Nevertheless the Devil, that irresistible seducer, prowled about the streets of their City of God. It was as though God was on the throne, but the Devil ran the government.

Before a historic consciousness could be born, much had to happen and many discoveries be made. The discovery, made by an élite, of a pre-Christian past was doubtless one of the more important; it conjured up a feeling of solidarity which permitted the living to recognise in themselves the successors to a vanished civilisation buried in the earth beneath their feet. For historic consciousness is primarily a comparative and critical awareness of that which is, and the wish to live in three dimensions of time; observing the past as though it still existed, and the present as though it were already past, seen as from the standpoint of the future.

The Renaissance discovered history in the gestures—examples which could be copied—of great men; the apostles and the saints had to yield their place to those whom they had eliminated long ago, to the heroes of Plutarch, to the philosophers of antiquity, to the scholars and encyclopaedists of Alexandria. The march towards the future was resumed in the guise of a search for the road towards the City of Antiquity. The City of God no longer existed, and with this extraordinary eschatological imposture ended the terroristic dictatorship of the Devil—not everywhere, however, nor for all time.

As for the Reformation, it too went back to original sources and re-established the eschatology of the Old Testament and of the Gospels of Jesus. Thomas Muenzer proclaimed the Kingdom of God. It was to be built without delay, and here on earth, through justice and equality. Everything belonged to everybody and everybody belonged to God!

The theocratic revolution was drowned in the blood of the Anabaptists and of those peasants who had just learned from the Gospels that the world belonged to them, and that they themselves owed obedience only to their Creator. This was the last of the revolutions in favour of God and intended to establish his reign; those who came after were to claim the rights of man and to speak the lay language. When on May 27th, 1525, Thomas Muenzer was shamefully put to death, God suffered His most terrible defeat in Europe. The idea that there might be a salvation without Him became thinkable. 'The Heavens belong to God, but He has given the earth to all the Sons of Man', and the sons of man proposed, in effect, to take their heritage and to put everything where it truly belonged; the sun and the stars in an empty sky, and time in its proper place. The need to know the truth about the past became a matter of urgency. It was necessary to conquer not only space and time, but all times, in order to be delivered of the weight of the past. The will of God, the secret intentions of providence? No, the search now was for an understanding of events, first of all through the actions, ambitions and errors of great men, then through the evolution of dominant ideas, and finally through the nature of man and the development of his various societies.

True historical thought begins as a critique of the religions, starting with those of other societies distant either in time or in space. As soon as religions are made objects of study, it is dis-

covered that they correspond to certain forms of society and that
these different social organisations seem to represent degrees of a
general evolution. If this is so, then history must, by definition,
be universal. Whereas it had previously been seen as a sequence
of war-chronicles and tales of catastrophe, of epics and of
gestures, it now becomes the history of societies and of civili-
zations. It reveals its true character, which is epic and not
dramatic. Were Homer to come back today he would learn a
great deal about Troy: that Troy was built upon soil that had
already swallowed five cities before his Mycenaean one, and after
that was to witness the building up and falling down of three
more. He would learn of the part that the Egyptians and the
Hittites had played in the war against the Trojans and would
discover that the expeditions of the Achaeans, those *Aquaiuchas,*
had been rightly considered as simple assaults by barbarians in
search of plunder. Homer would be astonished to learn how many
thousands of years lay behind him, and even more so that those
millennia exist for us, that they are now within the reach of our
hands and eyes. For modern man is the first to have conquered
the past and to have integrated it into his *Weltbild,* his vision of
the world.

When conceived dramatically time's dimension is the length of
an act, it is linear; when conceived epically, in the history of
societies, it becomes spatial. The accomplished act survives in the
new situation, implying all that has gone before, thanks to the
Hegelian *Aufhebung* which is simultaneously the elimination and
the integration in time. Humanity is thus a river without a mouth
carrying with it all that has fed it and all that it has fed, since its
source.

It is never certain that any one man truly belongs to his age,
but it is certain that all men participate in all the epochs which
have preceded and prepared their own. Even without profound
analysis a psychologist would discover in each man and woman
the perpetuity of assimilated time.

For the last one hundred and sixty years or so in the countries
of Europe (and of European civilisation) there has existed a
generalised consciousness of living inside history: major events are

examined and immediately perceived as stages towards effects still far in the future, as promises made to that future as well as replies to the past. This implies an awareness that every social act is likely to have consequences reaching far beyond the village, the country or the continent. History has become global and concerns the entire world.

For the last hundred and sixty years the politician has wished to set himself up as an ideologist, and the ideologists have resisted with difficulty the temptation to take part in political life. The right wing intellectuals, basing their arguments on their knowledge of government and of administration, have dreamed of teaching the great how to increase their power and to ensure its permanence, while making the state stronger, order more stable and the governed more contented. They have all wished to be the directors of their princes' political consciences, to be Grey Eminences.

It was with the French Revolution that intellectuals as such first obtained power. They knew precisely what must be done in general, and they found themselves compelled to improvise what they would do tomorrow. From the old Roman Republic they borrowed the gestures and the rhetoric of virtue, but the Declaration of the Rights of Man opened a new era. By asserting that the liberty of the human person is inalienable, they established that no institution could ever claim to be superior to man.

Later these ideologists-in-power instituted a reign of terror. The jails were crammed with political prisoners and the guillotine decided the quarrels of factions. The Revolution committed suicide. The more cunning careerists survived, still young enough to rise with the Consulate, to prosper under the Empire, and to ensure a fine future for their children under the Restoration. After all, regardless of ideology, there is no novelty in the fact that the Fouchés become high functionaries and the Saint-Justs young corpses. Since that Revolution whose defeat was but an episode, but whose victory was an event for more than a century, the left wing intelligentsia has wished to be revolutionary, has seen itself entrusted with the mission of transforming history by means of dramatic actions. Neither Hegel, nor the French socialists, nor

Marxism, is explicable without this Revolution which can be
described as the glorious, if clumsy, application of a philosophy
which had not then been formulated in terms other than those of
an eschatology.

3

The first German revolution had been religious, but the second
was philosophical, a cataclysm in the universe of ideas. Kant,
denounced as dangerous to the order, religion and dynasty of
Prussia, replied that among other virtues his writings had that of
being incomprehensible to the mass of the people. A causalist, he
conceived human evolution as being determined by the laws of
human nature and by the necessities of society. (If he refers
occasionally to the 'intentions' of nature, this is a literary, and
certainly an opportunistic, turn of phrase.) His fundamental
datum was that antagonism which he defines as the 'unsociable
sociability' (ungesellige Geselligkeit) that marks the present,
immature state of humanity.

However the Enlightenment on the one hand, and the terrible
dangers inherent in modern warfare on the other, would push
humanity to choose at last the way of reason leading towards the
republic and towards universal peace. Lao-tze and Confucius,
Plato and his like, had sought the answer in the wisdom of
government [1]; Kant, and in this he resembles Spinoza, found it in
the advancement of the human race towards wisdom. The
philosopher of Königsberg was a progressive, not a finalist, as
Darwin was to be in biology; the idea of time having an end was
for him inconceivable and fundamentally ridiculous; he lived
decidedly outside the realm of eschatology.

[1] Some Chinese writer should write a novel, a great philosophical and
humorous work, about Confucius and his search for the prince who
would give him his high office for a year or two—just to prove.... And
what a wonderful hero Hobbes would make for an English novel, the
conservative eternally embroiled in a revolutionary's troubles!

In 1798, at the age of seventy-four, he announced that the French Revolution, despite its errors and crimes, was a good proof of the general tendency of the human race towards progress and towards a universal republic.

In 1792, Hegel, then aged twenty-two, was studying theology at Tübingen, as did almost all the philosophers of that period in the early stages of their careers. He became a close friend of Schelling and of Hölderlin, even sharing a room with them. He too was enthusiastically in favour of the Revolution. He wrote: 'Since the sun first appeared in the firmament and the planets began to revolve about it, nothing like this has ever been seen: man is standing on his head, that is to say relying upon his ability to think, and is constructing a world accordingly . . . This has been a magnificent sunrise. Every being capable of thought has rejoiced in this epoch. An immense emotion, an enthusiasm of the spirit, has caused the universe to tremble, as though at this moment the Divine and the Universal were reconciled.'

He was constantly re-reading Rousseau, who had a most profound influence upon him. Most of what he wrote before *The Phenomenology of Spirit* deals with politics. (The exceptions being a mediocre poem and an essay on love.) And when for the first time he and Hölderlin parted they chose as their motto: 'The Kingdom of God!'

Hegel belonged to his age, and he was to change even as it did. His political evolution might be described as 'coincidentalist': during the Revolution a revolutionary, under the Emperor (that *Weltseele* or soul of the universe) Hegel became a Bonapartist. With Napoleon's defeat he was to turn to Prussia, whose state promised him the supreme achievement of history—precisely the 'idea as it is realised on earth.' It is true that he did not declare in 1830 that 'the soul of the universe' was now Frederick Wilhelm II, but by then history no longer needed 'persons of universal history' (*Weltgeschichtlich*). In Hegel's work the *Weltgeist* had finally achieved absolute knowledge, and had realised itself in both senses of that word. When the news of the July Revolution reached Berlin the philosopher was worried and irritated to such an extent that even a hand of cards failed to restore to him that sublime gaiety which his friends at the card table had learned to expect. This new event was inconceivable, coming far too late, *post ultimum actum*. Similarly the Whig Reform Bill of 1832 was in his eyes a perverse phenomenon. Hegel proved this in articles that he wrote for the *Official Journal* of Prussia.[1]

Socrates, Luther, Dostoievsky and Nietzsche are also worrying cases: each of these provided the explosive material needed to overthrow the existing hierarchy of values and to cast down firmly established social superstructures; and each was to live long enough to justify finally that which he had begun by destroying. All the same, the case of Hegel would be the most astonishing of all if we were to overlook one surprising and extremely rare fact: this genius was a fool. Now it is true that folly is to be encountered with a greater relative frequency in run-of-the mill philosophers than in, say, cabinet makers, but nevertheless one hardly expects to find genius and folly combined in a thinker as one might, for example, in a great painter. Hegel, more than any other man, has given currency to this sort of folly 'in depth' which has recently proved so acceptable to certain French philosophers—notably those who, being ontologists and lacking any real relationship with such a system, have discovered themselves to be Hegelians in order to convince themselves that they are really revolutionaries.

Hegel's pages on the master and the slave, perhaps a little over-quoted, contain what might be described as the elements for a philosophic *aria*. No other man either before or since the author of the *Phenomenology of Spirit* has been so successful in showing dialectic as the mode of 'becoming', as a movement of thought and as a didactic method. And curiously enough it is in these very pages that is to be met most frequently the poetic glow and the Hölderlinian mode of expression.

His argument is based upon one postulate: that the slave became enslaved because he preferred life to struggle. And though this may happen in individual cases, in general and speaking historically this statement is utterly false. It is one of those ancient

[1] Their violence of tone was such that even the *Official Journal* of Prussia could not bring itself to publish them.

lies with which all dominant classes have sought to prove their legitimacy. Similarly the very fine conclusion (about the power of work to mould and to set free) is in part astonishingly banal and in part wrong. To prove this it is only necessary to refer to what Marx and Engels wrote on this same subject, passages in which they finally put an end once and for all to such philosophic obscurantism. (What Hegel has to say about women, marriage and children is equally unconvincing.)

What is most distressing about the more ambitious flights of spirit voices from beyond the grave is, as we know, the fact that they make the towering dead speak exactly as if Buddha and Aristotle, Caesar or Napoleon, had possessed precisely that degree of intelligence and those somewhat limited scholarly recollections which we find in professional spiritualists.

Hegel's work resembles a spiritualist séance in that it is the dialectic autobiography of the *Weltgeist* composed at the moment when that *Geist* has reached the end of its long voyage called universal history—at the moment when this spirit of the universe has finally achieved absolute self-knowledge. How then are we to avoid astonishment at the ignorance of its own being which this spirit manifests on every page of its autobiography? Indeed the philosopher, extremely widely read at least during his youth, knew considerably more than did the *Weltgeist*; but this latter, a Hegelian of the strictest sort, was compelled to ignore such matters as, for example, what the philosopher had learned from the intuition of Edward Gibbon, whom he had read most thoroughly.

The *Weltgeist* says: 'I was in the East among those who knew that one man was free; later I was with the Greeks who knew that some men are free. And now I have reached my home, among the Germanic peoples who know that all men are free.' What luck for Georg Wilhelm Friedrich H.: he found himself in the right place at the right time, a German and a Berlin professor precisely during the twenties of the nineteenth century. Finally summoned to the capital by the King of Prussia, in his inaugural address Hegel attacked Kantism and the Enlightenment in the most violent terms. He spoke of Kant's ignorance and platitudes, of his pride in having forgotten 'higher interests', of his self-satisfaction derived from knowing nothing about the eternal and the divine, etc, etc. By 1818 it was high time to put the affairs of the mind in order and to be done once for all with agnosticism and criticism. It was time to consolidate the victory of the counter-revolution.

Hegel a counter-revolutionary? He who was the first to insert into a total, logical system liberty of conscience, not in the style of garrulous ideologists, but in the revolutionary sense—as real conquests? Hegel, who refused the hypothesis of man's submission to fate, and who recognised in him the carrier and the creator, not the victim, of a magnificent and exciting destiny?

That which is usually important in the work of the very greatest philosophers, is the question which they were the first to ask, and almost never the answer that they provide. Lesser thinkers can, at best, find another way, a relatively new form, in which to put a question which is already too well known. And in most cases the answers that such men provide are totally irrelevant. More often than not philosophy is a labour of Penelope.

Let us imagine Hegel dying during that night of October 1806, on the eve of the Battle of Jena, when he had just written the last lines of his *Phenomenology of Spirit*: 'History understood (conceived) constitutes the memory and the Calvary of the Absolute Spirit, the reality, the truth and the certainty of its throne, without which it would be an inanimate and solitary being . . .' He then added two further lines taken from Schiller's poem on friendship, of which the very last word of all is: 'the infinite'. Had he died on that night, he would not have been there the next morning to see the Spirit of the Universe riding on horseback through the streets, nor would he have been able in the years to come to proclaim the end of history. He would have bequeathed to us the supreme anxiety engendered by his bold questions, and he would have spared us the great number of his certainties, sublime in their audacity, stupid in their relationship with reality. And Mussolini, Hitler and Stalin would have had to do without this foreshadowing of a system which, in the terms of a liberating and final revolution, justifies the institutions of totalitarianism and, in effect, stands everything on its head: a system in which liberty becomes slavery, emancipation submission, loyalty alienation: where the *Weltgeist* is incarnate in the despot, and absolute conscience is manifest in an infamous and omnipotent police, or as he said 'the reality, the truth and the certainty of the throne' of the Absolute Spirit.

Up to now no worse reactionaries have been seen than those revolutionaries who have achieved power and who then order everyone to conform to the state of affairs which suits their type of government. Within a remarkably short length of time such men resume in their persons and their actions all the filth handed down from the past. Mystifiers in power are the cruellest of tyrants, for they are not satisfied that truth should keep silent. They insist that it should die, crushed beneath the throne of the Absolute Lie.

Faced by a philosophy which claimed to be the final reconciliation of the idea and of the reality, Marx, as a young man, began by being the spokesman for a great philosopher who has been strangely neglected for many years, Ludwig Feuerbach. It was from him that Marx learned the two critical truths which, in addition to Jewish eschatology, were to be the very foundation stones of Marxism:

1. Philosophers confuse the subject and the predicate, mistaking the one for the other; but none has ever pushed this confusion as far as did Hegel, for whom the real man, the real family and real society, are only predicates of which the subject is the state.
2. The story of alienation, being based on this same confusion, simply records the accidents of abstract thought, thus obscuring the true phenomenon, which is the auto-alienation of real man.

Marx thought of himself as a critic. His most characteristic works contain the word 'critique' in their titles. (A reminder of Kant's books.) At the age of twenty-three, in 1841, he embarked upon a programme of demystification, with his *Critique of the Hegelian Philosophy of the State*; he continued it with his *Critique of the Hegelian Philosophy of the Law*, and concluded it with his *Political Economy and Philosophy*. This last work, only discovered in 1931, is in part a critique of *The Phenomenology of Spirit,* and in part a first outline for what was later to become his *Critique of Political Economy.*

Marx was still expressing his ideas in that 'philosophic phraseology', as he was to admit a little later. (Certain Hegelian mannerisms were to remain with him until the end of his life.)

Marx was to maintain later that he had found dialectic standing on its head, where Hegel had put it, and that he had placed it back upon its feet. But no change is possible within Hegelian philosophy. Dialectic is not only its method, but also its content, and is precisely that element of it which is concrete in the way of all true idealistic philosophy. In Marxism dialectic is the general method of all movement, the law that governs every sort of evolution. It only becomes concrete in science, when it is applied to the real world. That is why 'it is necessary to escape from philosophy and to devote one's studies to the real world ... Philosophy is to the study of the real world what onanism is to sexual love', as Marx wrote in his *German Ideology.* For philosophy is not a suppression of auto-alienation but on the contrary is its means and its characteristic mode of expression; whereas the materialistic critique, insofar as this is a 'real humanism', becomes by 1844 the consciousness that an antagonistic reality acquires of itself, a step towards the final emancipation, a terrible force once it has gained control of the masses. It is social reality that determines man's conscience, and not his conscience that determines reality. Now this reality, Marx pronounces, has entered into its final state of contradiction. The capitalists like the proletarians are living in a state of auto-alienation. But the bourgeois, to achieve freedom from this, should lose his wealth, whereas the proletarian has nothing to lose save his chains. His class is the only one in history which needs no mystification, for in making his revolution he is seizing power not in order to keep it but in order to abolish it for ever. A victorious proletariat will not assert its right as a dominant class, but will destroy itself along with all the other classes. Realised morality is not, as Hegel had taught, the total state, but quite the contrary: the total disappearance of the state. 'For Hegel man is but the state subjectivised; for democracy the state is but man objectivised,' Marx says at the beginning of his critique. A little later he was to learn that there exists an incompatibility between the state and the man who has been emancipated, that is to say 'disalienated'.

Feuerbach, the French socialists and the English economists provided the newly born Marxist system with that arsenal of critical weapons which it expected to use in due course to win its permanent and final revolution. Knowing the historic law, the next step for Marxism was to apply it in a series of actions which would transform the world and accomplish the final reconciliation of reality with conscience.

The *Communist Manifesto,* written in January of 1848, declares: 'Pauperism is growing even more quickly than population and wealth ... The bourgeoisie is henceforth incapable of remaining the dominant class of society ... The German bourgeois revolution can therefore be only the immediate prelude to a proletarian revolution.'

This revolution, the rumbles of which were already audible when Marx was beginning to write the *Manifesto,* took place. He was very soon disillusioned of all the hopes that he had placed in it.

From 1848 until our own time Marxism, insofar as it was set up as a scientific prediction of what was to happen, has suffered, in the course of an inexorable evolution, one long series of similar disillusions. But a failure that manages to endure for more than a century easily comes to resemble a triumph of mind. Marxism is neither the sole, nor indeed the first, example of this.

4

For just one century, that is to say since Karl Marx's time, the left has drawn sustenance from a 'scientific' certainty based upon a conception of history, upon a method of sociology, and upon the application of the so-called dialectical system. Aware of the inadequacy of moral arguments in social struggles, the intellectuals have adopted Marxism as the scientific explanation of all history, and as a means of rational action upon society in order to lead it away from the realm of need and to guide it towards the realm of freedom.

If one definition is accepted, all becomes convincing: *history is nothing save what man has produced by man's work, is nothing but what nature becomes for man.* Through a countless series of successive antagonisms, humanity has ascended to the final antagonism: that between the means of production on the one hand and social relationships on the other. The last phase of pre-history is with us. Marxism pretends to prove this as much by what it teaches as by what it is: the full historical awareness which is possible only at the end—which has now been reached—of a class society.

In 1848 Marx thought that capitalism had reached its end; that henceforth it could be only an obstacle to the development of productive resources; that absolute pauperization, *Verelendung,* would become the fate not only of the working class but of all the various social levels excluding only a tiny group of capitalists; that the proletariat had been definitely expelled from the body of the nation, detached from its Fatherland, and that it must remain so until the revolution had succeeded, when being the absolute majority it would itself constitute the nation; that from now on the immediate interests and the final interests of this class would be completely identified, so that the proletarian conscience could only be revolutionary: it had nothing more to lose, but the whole world to win.

In the sixty-five years between 1848 and 1914—which marked the real beginning of our century—Marxism was born and grew throughout the world, while at the same time capitalism developed with a rhythm hitherto unknown. The consequent economic and social changes contradicted in the clearest possible terms Karl Marx's basic predictions.

The following table,[1] which shows the industrial development of the more advanced countries, proves this:

The Development of Industrial Production: 1913 = 100

Year	Germany	France	Great Britain	Russia	United States	World Production
1860	14	34	26	8	8	14
1870	18	44	34	13	11	19
1880	25	53	43	17	17	26
1890	40	62	56	27	39	43
1900	69	79	66	61	54	60
1910	89	85	89	84	89	88
1913	100	100	100	100	100	100

Between 1850 and 1909 the real mean salaries (based on the prices prevalent in the period 1925/1934) increased in France from Fr. 6,760 to Fr. 14,420. In Germany, between 1851 and 1913, from RM. 1,520 to RM. 3,116.

The concentration of capital which Marx had correctly foreseen made great progress, but without entailing the consequences that he had drawn therefrom; the intermediate social classes between the bourgeoisie and the proletariat did not disappear; their proletarianization did not take place. Indeed, though since 1880 the numbers of the proletariat have increased absolutely, during this same period the numbers both absolute and relative of white collar employees and officials have increased more rapidly still. The tertiary sector of society (to use Colin Clark's phrase) has not ceased during this period to acquire an ever-growing importance.

The Great War proved that the proletariat did not feel excluded from the nation, and that this class thought that it did have something to defend when it fought for its country. This was a

[1] Given by Fritz Sternberg in his *Kapitalismus und Sozialismus vor dem Weltgericht* (Bund-Verlag, Cologne).

cruel blow to Marxism and to the International, its organization. In Germany the Social Democrat deputies, the representatives of the model Marxist movement, unanimously voted in favour of war credits. 'It is not true, not possible!' cried Lenin. 'This copy of *Vorwärts* which tries to tell us that it happened is no doubt a forgery put out by the Berlin Government!' But there was no denying the evidence; everywhere the proletariat had shown itself 'its people's finest son'. Then there occurred to Lenin, and to certain other revolutionaries isolated from the true working class, that idea which always emerges when a man refuses to recognise the basic reason for an unexpected defeat: the only possible explanation for what had happened was treason. The rank and file of the Party were doubtless loyal to the decisions taken in their name by the International at Stuttgart and at Basel, but the leaders had been corrupted by the bourgeoisie, and relying on a minority of workers demoralised by good wages they had betrayed the cause, the Party, the people.

No man could have been less well placed than Lenin to formulate such an explanation. The leader of the Bolsheviks had indeed never had anything to do with the masses and had never based any of his hopes on their political consciousness; on the contrary, he had always relied on action by an élite of professional revolutionaries which, being the only people possessing historical consciousness and being able to see beyond immediate needs and interests, would indefatigably pursue the final aim.

In choosing the thesis of treason, Lenin was looking for reasons which would enable him to remain faithful to the Marxist schematic even while he abandoned it. According to Marxism, one social class can betray another to which it is allied—for example, the bourgeoisie in the German towns of the sixteenth century, by not giving its full support to the peasants in their struggle against the nobility, compromised its own hopes of emancipation. By acting thus a class shows that it is not yet ready to assume its historic rôle. There are times when the leaders can play a part, and their virtues and defects are then of importance, but this can never be decisive. For after all it is the real and existing conditions which cause these leaders to emerge, and which impel them towards glory or failure. Seen in this perspective a leader's betrayal simply reflects inadequate circumstances.

'The masses must themselves know what they have to do and how they have to do it. This is an essential historical condition for social democratic action, even as ignorance on the part of the masses has been the essential condition for action by the ruling classes', wrote Rosa Luxemburg. 'Thus any distinction between the leaders and a majority following behind is abolished; relationships between the masses and their chiefs are reversed.'

During the summer of 1914 Marxism found itself face to face with the truth: the living proletariat did not resemble the theoretical proletariat, for the situation that developed was not the one that should have arisen according to the Marxist schematic. Marxist methods should have been applied to this mistake, and an attempt made to explain why, in the greatest holocaust that the world had seen, the front lines did not divide the classes but ran along the national frontiers. Instead the exact contrary was done. Error was elevated to the status of dogma; and a great gulf was dug between the idea and the practice. Thus they set off upon the *via sacra* of absolute falsehood.

Since 1914 the Marxists have based their hopes less and less on the class struggle and more and more upon the after-effects of war: on the material, social and moral decay that wars engender, and on the fatal weakening that authority suffers when it endures military defeat.

The revolution of February 1917 was not organised by any proletarian party. The October Revolution was only to be justified in Lenin's eyes by the proletarian revolution which should follow in the great industrial countries, and which did not take place. The revolutions of the winter of 1918 in the countries of Central Europe were the effect and not the cause of terrible military defeats. In most of these countries nationalist insurrections dominated social uprisings. The Russo-Polish War of 1920 provided yet another proof that the national factor took precedence over that of class. Finally, nationalist mysticism won the day everywhere—in Italy, in the Balkans, in Germany, and in Stalin's Russia.

Throughout the Second World War Fascism and anti-Fascism fought one another beneath the flags of an exaggerated nationalism, and no matter which side it was on, each of the nations involved appealed primarily to the patriotism of its citizens. The resistance movements, it is true, spoke much of liberty and of democracy, but the only concrete meaning that they ascribed to these slogans were national liberty and independence. The Comintern floundered from one rebuff to another beneath the slogan of 'Class against Class'; in several countries the Communist Parties only became a real factor in political life when they organised a Popular Front and formulated a national democratic policy. Later, during the resistance, they became the active left wing of a ferocious nationalism which now called itself the National Front.

Despite all these events, the Marxist schematic was not revised but only slightly modified, and even this was not publicly admitted. It became an ideology playing in fact the rôle of a liturgy, and the Communists utilised, according to their tactical needs, this or that part of it; the texts had by now become simple pretexts.

'The history of all societies up to our own day is the history of the struggle between the classes.' But the problem is whether the class struggle does or does not explain the global wars of our own century. In order to demystify men's minds, nothing is more urgent than to discover the mystery behind modern war.

Lenin, re-echoing the arguments of the German Social Democrat Hilferding and of Hobson, explains global war as follows: the new phenomenon, of which Marx was unaware for obvious reasons, is Imperialism, the last state of capitalism and the fomenter of wars. It is the struggle for raw materials and for markets in colonial or semi-colonial countries, the imperialist competition of finance capital to acquire by military means the possibilities for investing in order to make super-profits. The decisive factor is the unequal stages of development prevailing in the various capitalist countries in the world. The classic example was the dangerous rivalry which existed in world markets when German capitalism came into competition with British capitalism.

Before the First World War the conquest of markets had become a vital question for German industry; hence the war between the Reich and the British Empire appeared, if not inevitable, at least logical. The involvement of France, of Russia, of the Hapsburg Empire and so many other European states, and finally of the United States of America, appears as an accidental or supplementary event, but not an inevitable one if the causes of the First World War are seen simply in the light of the Hilferding-Lenin explanation. (Outside, and indeed despite, this logical system Lenin regarded Russian expansionism as a particularly dangerous form of Imperialism.)

We know that the result of this war was the creation of numerous national states, that is to say the splitting up of markets and not the enlargement and unification of huge fields of commercial exploitation beneath the control of this or that victor. Within a very few years of her defeat, Germany, supported and effectively helped by her Imperialist conquerors, began to resume and indeed skilfully to perfect her industrial output, and to augment greatly her industrial potential. Foreign loans and investments amounted to some twenty-five billion marks. Germany re-exported or invested some ten billions. In 1929 her industrial production was greater than it had been in 1913, that is to say in the period when Alsace-Lorraine, the Saar and the industrial areas later ceded to Poland had still formed part of the Reich. Ten years after the war, this defeated Imperialist country was exporting as much as before the war that was supposed to have eliminated her from world markets once and for all. So what had been the purpose of that war? And what is the madness that afflicts these Imperialist masters of our world?

Shortly after the 1914 war it became apparent—and this is a point on which the Marxists rightly insist—that the real imperialist contradiction should not find Great Britain opposed to Germany but to the United States, for about 1880 America had taken its place in the first rank of world producers and since that date had not ceased to outstrip the other imperialist countries. On the seven seas and all the continents America has become the heir to the British Empire. According to the Marxist theory of imperialism, conflict between these two forms of capitalism is inevitable. However, in both World Wars as well as in the present crisis, the only certain alliance has been that which unites these two obvious rivals.

For the Stalinists, the Second World War was an imperialist one desired and launched by the French and British bourgeoisies. As of June 22nd, 1941, it was transformed into a peoples' war, a war of the peoples fighting for their liberty against Hitler. This metamorphosis was even retro-active. The Great War became a patriotic war too, and Foch, Galliéni and Mangin, among others, were judged worthy to appear on the placards of the Stalinist party in France.

But the most remarkable fact of all is doubtless this; neither in the First nor in the Second World War did the proletariat play a decisive political rôle. It had the weight of its mass, and nothing more. It had neither prevented wars, nor decided how they should end, nor imposed a peace which corresponded in any way whatsoever with the principles of proletarian internationalism. Such political bankruptcy is partly explicable in terms of the functions that the worker performs in modern war: he is no longer the man who suffers the most, he is no longer cannon fodder. The industrial proletariat makes the weapons of war, but uses them in battle less and less. It is from the peasantry and from the middle classes of the nations that soldiers are now recruited, rather than from the factories.

Engels, observing the results of general elections in Germany, wrote: 'Today one soldier in five is a socialist. Within a few years the figure will be one in three, and by about 1900 the majority of the army will consist of socialists. This state of affairs is approaching as inevitably as fate. The Berlin Government must see it coming even as clearly as we do, but there is nothing that it can do about it. The army is escaping from the government.'

No, Engels was not a simple-minded man; in fact he was less naïve than any other Marxist, and he was the first to foresee that wars in our century would be total. But he refused to recognise, even as Kautsky, Rosa and Lenin were to do, that there was an infra- and super-structural process at work: the workers, even while they were being organised as conscious proletarians aware of belonging to a class, were becoming increasingly integrated into society, and were turning into the lower middle class; escaping thus from the Marxist eschatology, they abandoned the perspective which saw an end to history.

Working class pacifism remains a real phenomenon and is more radical than petty bourgeois pacifism. But the statement that peace is infinitely preferable to war is simultaneously the most true and the least effective statement in the world.

If the working man has failed to play the historic part assigned to him, so has the bourgeois. The master, the captain of industry, the superman of the joint stock companies, was seen to collapse miserably in the great crisis of 1929 and the years that followed. When the storm burst, the giants of Wall Street were observed to behave like babes lost in the wood. The specialists in their employ wrote psychological treatises on the economy, and went on to advise the unemployed to sell apples at street corners.

In our century the ruling classes have launched wars which they had completely failed to foresee, and as a result have fought them with an incompetence that has proved both murderous and suicidal. Victorious, they have been unable to profit from their triumph which, from the very first day, has looked like the nightmare that it should only have become on the second day. The technique of the engineers and the organising skill of the managers have surpassed themselves to create miracles of efficiency, but these miracles of efficiency have been placed at the service of policies whose progress resembles that of spastics guided by blind men. Here, then, is a century in which everyone knows everything, and yet in which mediocre men such as Hitler or Stalin are considered as figures of genius and a Roosevelt as a statesman without a peer. The epigones of a German philosophy, itself epigonic, have become specialists in the General Strike, busy explaining to the workers what is meant by proletarian man, while persons like Joe McCarthy are the defenders of our liberties.

The nineteenth century produced the ideologies: the twentieth put them to the proof in the only serious way, namely by living

them, and dying for them. And by killing them. It is high time
that the word ideology be once again invested with that pejorative
sense that Marxism gave it long ago. It is also high time that those
men who would interpret facts without knowing them, like
eunuchs giving lessons in the art of love, should at last fall silent.

The failure of the Marxist schematic is thus written clear in the
events of the last hundred years and in the facts visible today.
The failure of the Marxist method has not yet been proved. All
methods employed in scientific researches in which man is
simultaneously the object and the subject, as for example in
psychology, are doubtful. Psychology began by making certain
'sensational' discoveries, but before long it was confronted by a
major difficulty: over-determination in psychic deeds and states.
It is not possible to limit, experimentally and by choice, the
number of conditioning factors, nor to foresee which of them will
become the decisive one. Psychology is unwearying in prophesying
from the past as soon as it has studied its result, the present, and
in proving that that which it knows has happened was bound to
happen absolutely. Whether a miser's son becomes himself a miser
or, on the contrary, a spendthrift, it is easy in either case to prove
post factum that his character was formed according to the
infallible laws of an interpretive psychology.

A grave economic crisis such as that which developed in 1929
creates a situation which is objectively revolutionary. It can
equally well result in a counter-revolution. As it went on, it
awakened a sense of profound discouragement among millions of
unemployed, to whom it gave the feeling that they had been
degraded. Instead of increasing, it diminished the number of
strikes, for the workers came to fear unemployment even more
than they feared capitalist exploitation.

The empiricist neglects this relationship between the being and
his consciousness, and fails to recognise the complexity and the
many dimensions of social existence; whereas the philosophical
idealist ignores what is concrete, and confounds the reflection
with what is reflected. Compared with them, the superiority of
historical materialism is not open to doubt. Is it not then a cause

of astonishment that it be almost never applied? It has inspired only a few historical works, usually brief essays, such as that by Marx on the Civil War in France, by F. Engels on the Peasant War, by F. Mehring on Prussia, by L. Hartmann on Italy. The historical works of Pokrowski, despite their weaknesses, are undoubtedly incomparably superior to all that Stalinism has produced—scarcely high praise. (Even the Middle Ages knew no such frenzy of falsification as that which has been imposed on the historians in the name of Marxism—Leninism—Stalinism . . .) Apart from Trotsky's *History of the Russian Revolution,* Marxism has so far failed to inspire a single great work of historiography. During the thirty years in which it has exercised an extraordinary attraction on intellectuals—most of whom have become the singers of litanies, the turners of Tibetan prayer-wheels—not one single work on politics or economics that can be assigned to the first rank has been produced.

Raymond Aron, in his introduction to *The Philosophy of History,* insists on the plurality of the fields of understanding in history. It would not be wrong to surmise that he reached this lucid position thanks to Marxism among other causes (as was incidentally also true for Max Weber and his school). Historical materialism is perfectly compatible with a pluralist method of research and of interpretation, as with every kaleidoscopic conception of human reality. That which has been lived (*Erlebnis*) provides in almost infinite variety the raw material of experience (*Erfahrung*): this experience is action, is the creation of special relationships between phenomena, and is consciousness of that social ensemble which each individual represents in himself, simultaneously the product and the producer of the conditions in which he lives: this is what historical materialism desires to understand, and to insert within the framework of the age. Marx and Engels insisted on the fact that men are mistaken about their own epoch and about the real effect of their own actions upon history. Like the psychologist, the historian must take into account these two fundamental data: (1) man is capable of making mistakes, and in certain conditions is incapable of not making mistakes. In order to escape from ignorance it is essential that man be aware of his ignorance. But he can ignore it. In order to achieve awareness his conscious has to conquer his unconscious. Like History according to Marx's definition, truth is a production of man by his labour: (2) Man perceives according to a system of relationships and references (Alfred Adler: *Bezugssytem*) and he acts within a limited field of action. Now if the act is less than the actor, it nevertheless reaches beyond the actor and beyond his field of action. Though limited in time, it is infinite in effect. The history of revolutions and of wars, like that of the designs and actions of the 'personalities of universal history', of Moses and of Jesus, of Alexander, of Caesar, of Luther and of Lenin, thus appear to be a tale told by an idiot ... The alienation between the intention and the action that it inspires—and which, once carried out, goes on endlessly—explains much, but does not explain itself except in psychological terms, which are insufficient for a sociological understanding.

Historical materialism postulates the study of social reality as the determining factor in the results of action, and it judges ideologies according to the function that they perform in reality. There has never existed a single form of government which did not claim that it had the highest and most admirable aims in view. The fraudulent promise of jam tomorrow is as old as oppression and as the massacre of the innocents. And there have always been a superfluity of ideologists available to provide the desired explanations; for example, even if such ideologists admit that in the U.S.S.R. one citizen in twenty is a slave labourer, they add that: 'no matter what may be the nature of present Soviet society, the U.S.S.R. is *grosso modo* on the side of those forces which are fighting against exploitation.' The quotation is taken from *Les Temps Modernes*, which went on to say: 'Every policy which is explicitly against Russia, and which localizes its criticism to her is an absolution granted to the capitalist world.' How so and why, since Soviet society today is by nature a totalitarian slave state, therefore quite definitely the opposite of socialism, and the rival, though not necessarily the opposite, of the Czarist or capitalist world? The director of this same publication, *Les Temps Modernes*, in order to put Camus in his place and to teach him

what a true rebel is, goes on to explain: 'We are therefore simultaneously against it (Stalinism) because we criticise its methods,
and for it because we do not know whether an authentic revolution
is not a pure chimera.' The logic of dupes or of impostors—*grosso
modo*?

So there we are. The left needs historical materialism more than
ever before; it needs it in order to reject such gentry once and for
all towards the right whence they come, towards that conformism
which today is leading them directly to Stalinism. The day that
the left agrees to judge governments according to their propaganda, their constitutions and their flags, it will be lost.

Some men embraced Communism precisely when it became
Stalinist, because they thought to find in it a church. They only
left it in order to join some other church. What have we in
common with them, those people who dare not face life if they
are not corsetted and protected by the armour of dogma?

Others left the Communist party without shaking off the
Stalinist police conception which had turned them into agents.
They have remained totalitarian in their thought and in their
methods, enemies of the left both of yesterday and of today, the
instruments of another power. Have we and they at least one
enemy in common? It cannot be said with any certainty. One
August day in 1939 we woke up to find that we and those
totalitarians who had been hitherto 'anti-Fascist' no longer had
an enemy in common. There is no reason to have any more faith
in the anti-Stalinist totalitarians of today.

Others again, and these are close to us, are in danger of going
wrong because they are unable to shake off the negative obsession
that Stalinism has become for them. Each day their conscience is
outraged afresh by its crimes, its obscurantism, its reign of falsehood. Now we who were anti-Nazis knew very well that Nazism
was not a point of departure, no, not even a negative one, towards
the solution of the real problems of our age; and this is equally
true today for Stalinism. We must not think against it, but think
outside and beyond it. In order to condemn it and to conquer it,
it must be considered in terms of the real world, of the necessities

and possibilities of our century; and it would be a cardinal error to consider our age in terms of Stalinism. It represents an enormous power, and doubtless a mortal danger, but it has at its disposal neither an ideology nor any theory; it simply bastardizes the one and the other to serve the most violent permanent publicity campaign we have seen since Hitlerism.

Obsessed anti-Stalinists are themselves as much the victims of this publicity as are those Stalinists who do not live behind the Iron Curtain. In order that it lose all its power, even its negative power, over us, it suffices that we should despise it—itself, its masters and its slaveries. Hitler could kill the anti-Fascists, but he never succeeded in conquering them, because even when victorious he did not manage to stop them from despising him basically— himself, his publicity and his terrifying power.

Hitler's National Socialism was one obstacle that had to be eliminated; Stalin's variety is another. Its conquest is not an end, but a means which will enable us to continue along the road towards an end. Let us then consider the needs and possibilities of our age, hidden but not transformed by totalitarianism and all its foulness.

5

Of all the revolutions that the world has ever seen, the only one to have established itself permanently and never to have doubled back on its tracks is the Industrial Revolution. Now, a hundred and fifty to two hundred years since its inception, we know that it is only just beginning. A century ago the depth and extent of its effects seemed to Marx extraordinary. The use of steam power in industry was then only beginning, electrical energy was still unknown, as were the importance of petroleum and the internal combustion engine.

Before that Revolution, humanity's struggle against nature was a defensive war, a long series of tiny stratagems whereby mankind attempted to neutralise nature's enormous power and to avoid being harmed by the vast forces she could unleash; the Industrial

Revolution conquered those forces and used them to forge arms for the purpose of conquering nature herself.

This Revolution created a global consciousness. The Roman Empire and China existed at the same time, but for all intents and purposes were non-existent to one another. The peoples lived, separated by the seas and the continents, as though on different planets. Now the oceans are links and not barriers. During the past few years humanity has become one world, disunited but nevertheless still one.

Before the Industrial Revolution the values of civilisation were fundamentally esoteric. They were defined, maintained and lost by the exclusion of the great majority of mankind. All that is invented and produced today is defined, maintained and transmitted by an appeal to the greatest possible majority, to everyone. In order to develop, industry must transform the inhabitants of the entire world into consumers. It is constantly creating new needs which are then rapidly spread throughout all layers of society.[1]

Favourable to, and favoured by, all the sciences, this Revolution has changed man's way of living and has increased the length of the individual's life—more than doubling the latter.[2] (Pseudo-revolutionary babblers and those high-minded persons who dislike technology have quite failed to perceive that this is a fact with immeasurable consequences.)

Finally it is the Industrial Revolution which has given us the means of learning about the past and of understanding its message better than hitherto. It has made possible that contemporaneity which has permitted the establishment of the imaginary museum of art, and has brought the most distant space almost within our ken.

Machines have not enslaved men. They have multiplied his strength, but without making him necessarily more intelligent nor wiser. But why should technology be expected to produce those results when all the religions and all the philosophies have failed?

[1] See *La Condition Ouvrière*, by Michel Collinet (Les Editions Ouvrières, Paris).
[2] See *Machinisme et Bien-être*, by Jean Fourastié (P.U.F.).

IMPERIALISM AND THE EXTERNAL PROLETARIAT

The Industrial Revolution is of European origin. Born in England and France, it moved eastwards, its rhythm accelerating in Germany and slowing down in the countries of Eastern Europe; it crossed the Atlantic and in the United States of America achieved an acceleration that was equalled nowhere else. In the other continents it has destroyed the traditional ways of life: in part, in half, or almost entirely. It has there discovered and exploited those natural resources which it needed, but it has given back little in exchange.

Lenin's view of an imperialism that would exploit more and more intensely both the cheap labour and the raw materials available in the colonial territories has been proved wrong by the facts. The 'capitalisation' of such countries has scarcely been intensified since the First World War, while their industrialisation has made only very unsatisfactory progress. In its relationship to the industrialised societies, the overwhelming majority of mankind represents what A. J. Toynbee has called the external proletariat; its own poverty, contrasting with the wealth of those others, both push and pull this external proletariat into our global history. It will not decide our destiny, but on the other hand our fate will certainly not be decided without that proletariat being taken into account.

The following table clarifies this situation:

	Annual Revenue per person (in dollars)	Annual consumption per person: cotton, wool, artificial fabrics (in pounds)	Daily expenditure of energy per head (in C V)	Average length of life	
				Men	Women
U.S.A.	554	29.01	37.6	62	66 (1939/41)
Gt. Britain	468	21.80	27.1	60	64 (1937)
U.S.S.R.	158	6.70	6.8	47	50 (1940)
India	34	4.37	0.5	27	27 (1931)
China	29	3.51	0.5	—	—

These figures date mostly from before 1939, but that they are still valid today is shown by the figures published by the United Nations for the year 1949. These figures are surely extremely eloquent:

Annual Income per Inhabitant (in United States dollars)

U.S.A.	1,453	South Korea	35
Great Britain	773	Burma	36
Indonesia	25	Pakistan	51
China	27	India	57

These figures serve to reveal the principal problem of our century and the basic task which confronts the Industrial Revolution, a task made all the more difficult by the fact that Free Europe scarcely exports any capital these days and indeed is herself a debtor. Nevertheless our continent has her part to play. Her industrial capacity remains superior to that of the Stalinist Empire, which is second only to the United States (though second by a considerable distance) in the field of industrial production. But the technical rationalisation of European industry remains inadequate and the division of the continent into national sub-units has a debilitating effect on all economic planning.

Europe has but recently emerged from one war to find herself threatened by another which, to judge by all the evidence, would be infinitely more destructive than any that has gone before. Having ceased to lead the world, she is sulking over her fate. The dream of Europe today would be to find a form of security which would last for ever, and to do so by escaping from a planet which she can no longer control—the sort of dream which typically appeals to those who regard themselves as having been maltreated by fortune. A middle class which hopes for the largest possible profit and the least possible risks, a working class which, no longer actively nationalist, has yet even lost the desire to think inter-nationally, intermediate social groups which, true to their nature, are reluctant to emerge from parochialism, these all combine to give a great many Europeans the feeling that they are far weaker than is in fact the case.

So if Europe is reduced to playing only a subordinate rôle, although still an extremely important one, we are left with America and with Russia. Russian economy combines two methods: the primitive accumulation of capital with the terrible hardships inherent in the over-exploitation of labour, and the authority of a state which owns all properties and all industrial undertakings and an immense mass of slave-labour. Since the employer, that is to say the totalitarian state, has annexed to itself every right, and since its workers, whether free or slave, can make no claims against it without this action being automatically castigated as a 'counter-revolutionary act', that is to say a hostile crime directed against the state, the Soviet economy combines the most favourable conditions for the exploitation of men. Nevertheless the figures show that these totalitarian exploiters are very far from obtaining the results which, in the eyes of certain people, would justify their crimes.

Indeed the net products of large scale industry, reckoned in international units and per head of the population, are calculated in Russia as follows: in 1913, 317; in 1928, 340; in 1936, 408.[1] The following table will serve to compare these figures with those of production in certain other countries:

	1913	1928	1936
United States	1,345	1,738	2,005
Great Britain	580	676	835
Japan	309	515	580
Poland	—	576	664
U.S.S.R.	317	340	408

One of those sophists who reckon too quickly on their readers' ignorance, attempts to prove that, thanks to the state planning and to the enthusiasm of the socialists, socialist productivity has

[1] *The Conditions of Economic Progress*, by Colin Clark (2nd edition). The term 'international unit' allows comparison to be drawn between national economies as well as between various branches of industry. Clark's international unit (I.U.) is the quantity of goods and services that could be bought in the United States during the period 1925-1934 (average) for $ 1.

made enormous progress. The figures he quotes are those for the increase of the net industrial product. Here are his figures: The net product of major industry, reckoned in millions of international units (I.U.) was as follows in Russia: 1913, 916; 1928, 1053; 1936, 2859.

These figures undoubtedly reveal a considerable degree of progress, but in order to form a true judgment of productivity it is obviously necessary to take into account the number of workers employed in these industries. These were, in 1913, 2,890,000; in 1928, 3,100,000; in 1936, 7,010,000. These figures will be more meaningful if they are compared with the equivalent figures in the United States. There, in 1913, 7,970,000 workers produced 10,730,000 international units; and in 1936, 9,140,000 workers produced, 18,330,000 international units.

Such statistics explain why in 1939 the net income per head amounted to $ 534 in the United States of America and to $ 158 in the U.S.S.R. (In analysing this data certain other facts must be taken into account, namely the effects of the Great War and, in the Soviet Union, of the civil wars, as of the Five Year Plans that began in 1928 and of the most profound and widespread crisis ever to affect the capitalist economy, which began in 1929.)

In the countries which she has conquered the U.S.S.R. has set up a form of imperialism based on booty and on the conversion of the vanquished, as was done by Hernando Cortes in Mexico and by the British trading companies in bygone centuries; but even if Russia were anxious to help Mao Tse-tung solve the Chinese problem, she could not do so. One example will suffice: in China, of seven hundred million acres which could be, at least in part, put under the plough, one hundred and seventy million are at present cultivated. The untilled soils are semi-arid. Despite the sceptisism of certain authorities, it is possible to image these territories being made fertile by means of modern methods, and notably by the use of tractors. It was the Soviet Union which in 1929 created the mystique of the tractor. Yet in 1950 Russia produced 108,000 of these machines, Great Britain 120,000, Western Germany 138,000 and the United States 541,000.

The revolution in China will be industrial or nothing at all.

Neither the abolition of the tenant system nor any other measure of agrarian reform can solve the agrarian problem, which is only one among many. Should Mao Tse-tung choose to follow it, the Stalinist road will prove even harder and far, far longer for the Chinese than ever it did for the Russians, who at least have vast natural resources at their disposal.

The primitive accumulation of capital plus slavery under a totalitarian régime, whatever name it may be graced with, will be an even more hopeless undertaking in China than elsewhere. In such circumstances that particular 'external proletariat' will be left with only one realistic prospect of self-betterment, namely a massive attack upon the industrialised world.[1]

With the exception of the United States, Russia was the only country to increase its rate of production between 1860 and 1913 in the ratio of 1 : 12.5; world production during this same period increased in the ratio of 1 : 7.14. The explanation is that the Czarist Empire imported foreign capital. This possibility no longer exists in our time, at least certainly not on the scale needed to fulfil the needs of China, and even less so if the aim is to satisfy the needs of Asia as a whole. The propagandists of the famous *free enterprise* system—of whom in the old days a number belonged to the left—are constantly urging private capital, in the most lyrical terms, to embark upon the great adventure. In vain. The 'monopoly capitalists' listen neither to their incantations nor to the laws of imperialism as formulated by the Marxists.

By 1937 the total product of the American economy had reached 228.2 billion dollars; of this 15.1 billions, that is to say 6.6 per cent, was exported. The amount of private capital invested abroad amounted to 700 million dollars, that is to say less than one third of one per cent of the total product. It should be further noted that since the First World War American exports have always been below one tenth of the national product: in 1919, 9.7 per cent, in 1920, 8.7 per cent, between 1921 and 1939 an annual average of 4.3 per cent, and in 1946, 4.9 per cent. American capitalism has developed in connection with an internal market of an astonishing expandability; the gamble of foreign

[1] See Jules Monnerot, *La Guerre en Question* (Ed. Gallimard).

investments offers no seductive appeal to the American capitalists. As a result they have no wish to be imperialists, and no need to be so. Whatever the noisy ideologists, echoing the totalitarian propagandists, may say, the legendary power of Wall Street which, at the beginning of this century, had a very real political meaning, no longer exists as such. In the Cold War this Street of Myth is if anything rather favourably inclined towards the U.S.S.R., just as large-scale German capital was between the two world wars. Wall Street would prefer to finance large-scale undertakings in Russia than invest its capital in India, for example, or even in Western Europe.

Less than 30 per cent of the population of the earth is actually living a contemporary life, that is to say living within the industrial society. It is obvious that neither private capital nor the efforts of a single power, even so rich a power as the United States of America, could undertake the enormous task of industrialising our planet within a reasonable period of time. No, capitalism is not dying; the rhythm of its technical development has been accelerated and not decreased; the so-called bourgeois sciences are making steady and constant advances. (The Soviet scientists are busily engaged in rediscovering that the inventions of the Western World were due to that extraordinary Czarist civilisation, misunderstood by all and notably by those who, after having first destroyed it, are now proclaiming themselves to be its proud heirs.) Nor does the fact that capitalism can never rid itself of social injustice (a state of affairs common to all previous societies) prevent that economic system from undertaking this great task. But the nature and the very scale of this gigantic initiative make it indispensable that all the national economies should cooperate on a global scale, should unite in an effort which far surpasses the capacities of any one of them. Since the Great War we have seen that a society, even though it has not abolished private property, is yet capable of planning its production, though this obviously implies that the owners of the means of production are not at liberty to dispose of those means entirely as they may see fit. The Second World War showed that even an economy as robust as that of the United States was incapable of satisfying the needs of the nation until the capitalist ceased to be sole master in his own house, and submitted to accepting state direction based on decisions which were not determined solely by the profit motive. This experiment was carried out in Great Britain and America without damage either to the liberty of the individual or to the right of free association: a centralised and even an authoritarian administration of the economy does not necessarily imply a totalitarian state. In those two countries the working class was thus able to make considerable advances and to increase, both relatively and absolutely, its share of the national income. Now, the industrialisation of the backward countries is as vital as the winning, or better still the avoiding, of a world war; it is indeed essential if we wish to abolish the external proletariat and thus to create the preliminary conditions for a political and social unification of our world.

The American bourgeoisie, heirs to one of the traditions of nineteenth century liberalism, and certain woolly-minded and confused idealists in Europe, are great publicists for the idea that it would suffice for the white nations to go home and leave the backward countries to their own devices in order to ensure their true emancipation. This is an attractive idea and shows generous sentiments, but it is inept. It is comparable to the thesis according to which a simple redistribution of land in countries such as Egypt would solve the problems that beset a massive peasant population. Agricultural reform, the elimination of feudalism and the final abandonment of that grotesque alliance which has existed between the Europeans and the local feudal nobilities, all such measures, even though they be reasonable enough, are ineffective, for without an industrial revolution the available soil is insufficient to nourish a population which is already far too great, and which is increasing at a truly hectic pace. To fight against any police despotism that the whites may impose upon the backward countries is far from bad; indeed it is morally very much in the interest of Europe that such a fight be constantly fought. But only by closing his eyes to the essential reality, can a man refuse to see the indispensable precondition to the real democratisation of such countries and to the ultimate suppression of their ruling castes and classes; for the final social and national emancipation of the backward peoples can only be brought about as a part of their integration, both as producers and consumers, into the industrialised world.

A man whom nobody could consider an extremist has formulated the only revolutionary programme in this connection to have been proposed for many years. In his message to the Congress, on January 20th, 1949, Harry S. Truman announced:

'We [the United States] must embark on a bold new programme for making the benefits of our scientific advances and industrial progress available for the improvement and growth of under-developed areas.

'More than half the people of the world are living in conditions approaching misery. Their food is inadequate. They are victims of disease. Their economic life is primitive and stagnant. Their poverty is a handicap and a threat both to them and to more prosperous areas. For the first time in history, humanity possesses the knowledge and the skill to relieve the suffering of these people ...

'We invite other countries to pool their technological resources in this undertaking. Their contributions will be warmly welcomed. This should be a cooperative enterprise in which all nations work together through the United Nations and its specialised agencies wherever practicable. It must be a world-wide effort for the achievement of peace, plenty and freedom ...

'The old imperialism—exploitation for foreign profit—has no place in our plans. What we envisage is a programme of development based on the concepts of Democratic fair-dealing.

'All countries, including our own, will greatly benefit from a constructive programme for the better use of the world's human and natural resources. Experience shows that our commerce with other countries expands as they progress industrially and economically.

'Greater production is the key to prosperity and peace. And the key to greater production is a wider and more vigorous application of modern scientific and technical knowledge.

'Only by helping the least fortunate of its members to help themselves can the human family achieve the decent, satisfying life that is the right of all people . . .'

But an appeal to common sense and to men's goodness of heart is not enough. At the time of writing, several years after this appeal was addressed both to the nations and to private initiative, it is plain to see that the results have been very meagre. It is only necessary to compare the vast sums of money, the human energy and the technical skill that the nations are prepared to spend upon their armaments, to compare the cost of one single day of total war with the cost of all that is being done for the backward countries, in order to realise how slight, and indeed ridiculous, an effort is actually being put into solving this immense problem, the most urgent of our age.

A left wing, truly aware of its purpose as well as of the needs and of the possibilities of the age, would everywhere be the spokesmen of a global solidarity, the unsilenceable advocates of Point Four, and would insist that every free nation should take part in this vast battle of construction by devoting to it ten per cent of the monies that it would risk losing in a destructive war. Such a left wing would give to the younger generation a mystique of active, international solidarity, and such emotions in their turn would evoke thousands of teams of specialists setting off for the backward countries in order there to build the bases of a true society, of a world really united by and in the work of emancipation.

If the greatness of an age can be measured by the size of the tasks that it sets itself, what epoch would surpass our own, were we to undertake this fruitful and productive transformation of the earth according to the needs of humanity?

It is the mobilisation and the creation of wealth that makes socialism possible—Marx quite rightly insisted on this point— and this is the exact opposite of the dissemination of poverty and the degradation of the individual in the name of the most abject tyranny.

Wars and Peace

Peace has never existed; what has gone by that name has been nothing but armistices of longer or shorter duration depending on relative strengths emerging from the previous war. The speed with which one armed conflict succeeded the last was determined by the speed with which that relativity of strength was altered during the armistice; a new holocaust took place just as soon as the equilibrium previously established was destroyed or seriously threatened either by developments inside one or more of the countries concerned or by a reversal of alliances. The peace treaties were sacrosanct for just so long as they reflected and expressed that relativity of strength; they broke down the moment that they appeared to guarantee certain advantages to one party no longer strong enough to defend them. (According to certain historians mediæval Europe was spared a multitude of great wars between the Christian states thanks to the spiritual harmony imposed by a powerful and authoritative church. In fact it was the extreme slowness of development during these centuries which enabled Europe to enjoy a long period of internal peace and of relative stability. War was exported outside the continent towards those areas which enjoyed a state of wealth unknown in a stagnant Europe.)

When societies are still at a primitive level the usefulness of war is obvious; killing men in order to eat them or to acquire possession of their land, of their water supply etc, is to make oneself their heir in order to live one's own life. Later it ceases to be necessary to kill the enemy in order to conquer him. Indeed at this stage it is advisable to kill as few enemies as possible, in order to obtain the maximum number of prisoners to work the land in the interest of the conqueror now installed in the territories of the conquered. This is almost the only type of war which can result in a true state of peace; as the years go by conquerors and conquered come to form one single nation, which in its turn will be united by wars fought in common against new invaders.

In more advanced societies wars lose their character of a vital necessity, and the mind begins to rebel against them. Civilised society becomes more aware of the terrible damage that they cause and less anxious to gain the frequently doubtful, and seldom durable, advantages that they bring to the victor. At the same time a false pacifism begins to appear, inspired by political or religious sympathy for the potential enemy—the one-way pacifism of the fifth column. To fight for one's country becomes 'to die for Danzig,' though the man who has said this will on the following day be prepared to fight for Hitler on the grounds that by so doing he is saving civilisation. Peace and coexistence at any price: but the day that Stalin launches an agressive war in Korea, such persons will seize the opportunity to launch a hate campaign against the United States of America. The words of Demosthenes have kept their meaning across the ages, for false pacifism is a phenomenon that shows a remarkable consistency.

Real pacifism has probably never prevented a single war. It is always at its most active in time of peace, and becomes by contrast extremely lethargic the moment that the clash of arms is heard—the only quality that it has in common with the muses. Its position is morally invulnerable and practically without effect, because it is based upon the conception that war is senseless and is the devil's work: it meanders on about diplomatic secrets, Machiavellian schemes, merchants of death, and so on and so forth. The pacifists, like most intellectuals, have not yet discovered that the development of force and what might be called the logic of power are real factors, that war is not essentially a psychological phenomenon nor an accident deliberately provoked in the relationships between communities. History is there to prove that the only means of ending, once and for all, armed conflict as the means of solving disputes between two sovereign communities is to merge them into one community. Nobody has feared a war between the French provinces since they were united into one indivisible state, just as no one now fears the outbreak of war between the Swiss Cantons or the States of the American Union. There were wars during that period of history when the parishes were being merged into the provinces, that is to say at the time when the nations were being born; during the stage when history is passing from national to continental unities, wars go on for just so long as any one nation claims the hegemony; unity is imposed finally when it has become a vital necessity and when hopes of hegemony have vanished in the face of a danger that threatens alike those who yesterday aspired to the mastery and those who yesterday, as today, refuse to be dominated.

There is nothing more revolting than the abominable choreography of the countless battles that have been fought during these past thousands of years, nothing more absurd than these endless massacres to prove ... what? Nothing more out of date than military pomp and military apparatus, nothing less compatible with our industrial society than these wars which themselves are in flagrant contradiction with the very essence of the Industrial Revolution that has made them possible.

It would be easy to add countless pages to the already vast literature written in these past few thousand years against war. They would be as reasonable as the wish to live and as useless as the refusal to die. Nevertheless, war is not the eternal fate of mankind, and it will disappear and become nothing but a memory, similar to those armed conflicts between the provinces that preceded the creation of the nations.

The Great War should have ended in the unification of Europe; the Second World War should have imposed such a unity. A mobilisation of the peoples for the purpose of European unity, such should have been the policy of the left. But the left accepted the policy of a division of spheres of influence, the scandal that permitted the greatest powers to impose the veto; and, being faithless to all its traditions, it failed to oppose the annexations, the deportations of whole populations, and so many other monstrosities. The left committed these terrible mistakes because it thought that it was its paramount duty to remain loyal to the conquerors, which involved also loyalty to that totalitarian power which had only been thrust into the camp of the anti-Fascists by the aggression of its Fascist ally. The left shared in every illusion and let pass without comment almost all the vile actions that were committed in the name of a victory which had immediately become the prisoner and the hostage of a tyrannical allied power. And yet the left should have known that a victory which means solely the defeat of the enemy is not the true way towards a real policy of peace, that it is valueless, and that it will eventually have to be rewon by means of new blood spilt in a new war.

Those dupes who act like impostors, and who are in any event certainly accomplices, cry aloud: 'Let us have peace! Let us negotiate!' Do they really believe that statesmen and diplomats create peace, are they unaware that such persons only translate the conditions of peace into juridical terms when they already exist? Well, they do not exist at present. By various means but with identical results the U.S.S.R. has seized the Baltic States, Poland, Hungary, Rumania, Czechoslovakia and Bulgaria, in addition to the annexed German territories and her Occupation Zone; she has destroyed the national independence of seven peoples and is busy exploiting their economy to the extreme, producing a poverty in those very products which they had in abundance before they fell into Russian hands.

In Europe annexations are the preliminary and invariable prelude to war. A man must needs be totally ignorant of politics and economics if he is to imagine, for example, that an ancient nation of seventy millions, situated in the very centre of our continent, gifted with a genius for work, and possessing technical skills in advance of all the other European nations, will resign itself to remaining the victim of cruel annexations. Only if he has failed to learn the most clearly pointed lesson of our age, will he fail to foresee that the national dynamism of the peoples will explode in a terrible revolution the moment that the totalitarian apparatus now exerted by the oppressors shall be sufficiently weakened. This apparatus, far from resolving the nationalist problems, has the effect of making them once again intensely topical and thus of resurrecting the purpose of the revolutions of the last century. An insane jingoism, brutally created wholesale by the police state, on the one hand persecutes Ukrainians and Jews, Poles and Hungarians, Czechs and Uzbeks and countless other peoples for their 'bourgeois nationalism', while on the other hand and simultaneously announces that to be internationalist means to be a Russian patriot, of the most violent sort. This government is systematically carrying out the total militarisation of the peoples over whom it exercises authority, while refusing to submit to any sort of international control, a control without which disarmament becomes quite impossible; para-military training is ordered for all, without exception; its propaganda is based on lies, on slanders against peoples, states and governments, on limitless perversions of the truth, and has the purpose of inspiring fear, hatred and contempt.

Exactly like Goebbels' machine, this propaganda accuses all those who do not serve Russia's purpose of being warmongers, militarist lackeys in the service of Wall Street, jackals and hyenas, rats and vipers. Every aggressive deed on the part on the Nazis was preceded, accompanied and followed by cries of: 'Long live peace! Down with the warmongers!' This hullabaloo failed to deceive the left; today it can only take in those who wish to be taken in. Otherwise they would have already perceived that it is the very men who wish to make war in detail, who in the most abstract terms proclaim themselves in favour of peace in general. Any man who pronounces war unthinkable, but is prepared to sign the appeals and resolutions of those who loosed the War in Korea, is a person of a remarkably mediocre political intelligence or else of a remarkably discontinuous sincerity, and he is making himself the instrument of the annexationists and of those imperialists who are out for booty. ('But how can the U.S.S.R. be an imperialist power, since it is a socialist state?—Precisely because it is not, neither *grosso modo* nor in any other way, socialist—But surely it is not capitalist?—No, it is not even capitalist. Nor were Pharaoh, Genghis Khan, or Ivan the Terrible capitalists in their time.')

The men of the right insist on identifying Stalinism with socialism and with the left as such, and would have us believe that, were it not for Stalin, the world would by now be finally enjoying both peace and happiness. But let us recall this simple fact: if Czarist Russia had remained one of the allies up to the victory of 1918 it would have engorged the greater part of the territories which Stalin annexed in 1939/40 and in 1945. It would undoubtedly have also strengthened its position in the Danube

Basin and would have seized considerable loot from the ruins of the Hapsburg and Ottoman Empires.

Colonel House, President Wilson's adviser and a man of astonishing political intelligence, expressed in the early years of the Great War his fear lest immediately after an allied victory Russia should become a terrible threat to freedom and to the independence of those peoples hitherto menaced by Imperial Germany.

Marx, for his part, wrote: 'Russian policy does not change. Its methods, tactics, manoeuvres may be altered, but the Pole Star of this policy, the domination of the world, is fixed.'

Russian imperialism has been a very real danger for centuries. It has always been a missionary imperialism (acting in the name of the Greek Orthodox Church, of Pan-Slavism etc) and has always been in search of plunder. It was not Stalin's invention. But the Soviet Union, being a totalitarian state, acts with technical means borrowed from the West in a period when the dream of world domination has become a practical possibility.

The left must struggle for the unification of Europe not simply in order to ensure our defence against a mortal peril, but also because the federation of our countries, while avoiding the hegemony of any one nation, is the only means of making wars between the European peoples an impossibility in the future. Such a federation is at the same time indispensable if the economy of Europe is to be rationally planned and permitted to assume its true rôle in the industrial development of the backward countries.

The United States of Europe will have to be created in conditions very different from those foreseen by the revolutionary Marxists before and during the First World War. None of them could envisage the political bankruptcy of the working class when confronted by the most urgent tasks, nor its apathy when faced with the possibility of realising that progress which its finest representatives and the most sincere nineteenth century pacifists were the first to formulate. At the beginning of the Great War Lenin launched an appeal to the working class (the so-called 'Seven Points') in which he demanded that that class 'transform the individual states of Europe into a republican United States.'

At the time of writing, this appeal has lost none of its validity; nor has another in which Lenin insisted upon the need for carrying out a 'pitiless and implacable struggle against Russian and Czarist monarchist Chauvinism.'

THE TOTALITARIAN STATE AND LIBERTY

It was undoubtedly during the Great War that certain individuals and ambitious groups learned a terrible lesson; men can be treated like so much manure, and their blood like so much fertilizer, to prepare the ground for the evil harvests to come: they can be regarded simply as means, as tools to achieve great ends. During that war generals were capable of sacrificing the lives of half a million of their own men in order to drive back the enemy's lines for a mile or two and to gain a few square yards of territory which must soon be lost again; was it, then, too much to sacrifice the lives of a few hundred thousand men and the liberty of a few millions in order than an humiliated nation might rise again, in order to transform the whole world, or even in order to improve the agricultural economy of a single country?

Should not the existence of conscript armies have threatened the traditional military system which is in essence authoritarian? If this prediction of Friedrich Engels has never been realised in practice, the reason is that military training was successfully used to destroy the soldier's individuality, to treat him as human material, to change a being with a conscience into the object and product of an absolute discipline. Face to face with the enemy, a company of soldiers is a community; face to face with its leaders, for example in a demand for an increase of pay, it becomes a mutinous assembly. It must be enthusiastically obedient, but without any will other than that inspired by a direct order.

It is the same story when a group of factory workers, assembled after their day's labour, enthusiastically votes that one month's wages be taken from them and loaned to the state. If on the other hand they meet together in order to express desires prompted neither by the state nor by the Party, they become criminals, at least according to paragraph 58 of the Stalin Code.

Totalitarian, like military, power aims to produce 'object organisations' submissive to its will, and to make impossible the appearance of 'subject organisations', that is to say communities with a free will. Two hundred million men faced by one million policemen are in a majority of two hundred to one, but all the time there is the single citizen-object, alone, without any sort of support, cut off from the entire world, and faced by a million omnipotent policemen who apparently rely on the support of the entire community minus one. These two hundred millions exist as humanity incarnate, but the moment that they disagree with the régime they are reduced, atomised, until they become nothing but a collection of solitary, abject and beaten criminals.

Thus all men belong to the state which itself belongs to the Party, but 'the Party organisation will replace the Party; the central committee will replace the Party organisation; and finally the dictator will replace the central committee.'

Thus wrote Trotsky in 1903, perhaps without really believing that such would be the evolution of Marxism. One year later Rosa Luxemburg wrote in *Iskra*: 'Socialism is the first movement in history to base its development entirely upon the organisation and independent action of the masses. The super-centralisation advocated by Lenin is not the deed of a positive and creative spirit but that of a negative and sterile spirit. His dream is to control the activity of the Party instead of bringing it to fruition; to restrain instead of expanding it; what attracts him is the rôle of the master, not that of the man who assembles and unifies.' [1] Fourteen years later in prison, Rosa was to give a prophetic sketch of the state of affairs later established beneath the rule of Yossip Vissarionovitch Djugashvili. In order that he might be everything, those two hundred millions must be nothing, while proclaiming day and night that they owed it all to him.

The obscurantism of that state is the most perfected that man is capable of creating. Its victims are imprisoned in an alienation which propels the individual even to hide his own thoughts from himself, to suspect himself, and to make his loyalty towards himself, his wife, his children, his parents and his friends, dependent

[1] Quoted from: *Three who made a Revolution* by Bertram D. Wolfe.

on the constantly changing but nevertheless absolute judgments of the state. It is insufficient that he should simply fail to disagree with those judgments, for silence itself is suspect; to be behind-hand in enthusiasm, to fail to cry quickly enough for the latest 'traitor's' death, is in itself at least a potential treason. A totalitarian government needs no censor; it will not allow silence, but insists on the entire population singing hymns to liberty in chorus.

Liberty, like justice and all the other great ideals, is first defined as the negation of a negation, in this case the absence of compulsion, of injustice and so on. True liberty cannot be defined in terms of the individual, but only in terms of the relationships of one individual with another, with groups, with institutions, etc. The 'reduction to objects' (*Verdinglichung*) of these relations seemed to the Marxists the last obstacle before the conquest of total freedom. They forecast that nothing would be opposed to the final liberation of everybody, once private property and private means of production had been abolished and the government of men replaced by the administration of things in a society which would be a free association of men liberated from every sort of domination and every sort of mystification.

No man can prove that such a state of liberty is a possibility; but what no longer requires proof is the fact that the Stalinist régime represents permanent and total counter-revolution, that is to say it is the ideal of the right; it alone is subject, since it alone owns men's bodies and souls and all possessions and means of production, since it alone is totally free, omnipotent. What-ever tactics, means and ideologies this state may employ in its internal or external politics, they are simply the interchangeable methods of pursuing one unchanging end: limitless power. The wish to dominate the world is inevitable for a government which cannot admit the existence of any opposition no matter what its form nor what its strength. Everything must become the anvil for a single hammer, itself. Even if, thanks to economic progress, it could one day lessen the terror, close the slave camps, abandon its methods of frenzied slander and of the disintegration of the

individual, it cannot and will not do so. Totalitarian power lives
beneath the compulsion of having to prove day and night that it
is what it is. It is revolutionary in the sense of Herostrates;
incapable of constructing a society, it is yet forced to destroy
everything that could form or constitute a social group outside or
apart from itself.

The anti-Fascists never pretended that there existed, beyond the
Fascist frontiers, a limitless liberty without any unpleasant
restrictions. Their policy was defined as 'against Hitler and his
satellites, and the localisation of criticism to these' but this did not
mean that they gave their absolution either to the capitalist world
or to the Soviet régime. They were engaged upon a struggle
against those assassins of liberty who seemed at that time to
constitute the greatest threat to mankind. Later the whole world
accepted their thesis, though by then it was virtually all over.
Neutralism, very popular while Hitler was a true threat, was
transformed into a pitiless anti-Hitlerism once Hitler had become
a pulverized corpse.

Many intellectuals who had been more or less inactive politically during the 'thirties' have embarked upon feverish anti-
Hitlerite activities, particularly once the Battle of Stalingrad was
won. They are in fact always one lap behind the totalitarians;
otherwise they would surely realise today that the danger against
which they should be fighting is Stalinist National Socialism.

No man save the Hitlerites and their fellows would have dared
to accuse us at that time of being indifferent to the sufferings of
the negroes, to the fate of the colonial peoples and of the slum
dwellers, to the misdeeds of the 'plutocrats'. Only the stupidest
or the most impudent of the Fascist intellectuals then said to us:
'Since you are against Hitler you must approve of the Ku Klux
Klan; you fight against us, so you are in favour of hindering the
unification of Europe; by pointing your weapons at us you prove
yourselves to be warmongers.'

It is true that we thought then just as we think now; that
liberty as practised in the democracies is very limited compared to
what socialism promises, but that compared to the conditions

existing under the Gestapo or the G.P.U. it is of enormous value and worth defending at any price. We are in favour of internationalism and of the abolition of all frontiers, but if unification is to be achieved by means of oppression and slavery, then national liberty is worth fighting for with all our strength. The independent trade unions, the right of association, freedom of opinion, the standard of living of the working class and of the peasants in the capitalist countries, such are some of the things that we unhesitatingly regard as worthy of defence against any totalitarian threat.

Even if totalitarianism were not threating all these values—relative values it is true, but real ones nonetheless—for the man of the left neutrality would still be in any event unthinkable. He has never accepted such states of coexistence; he has never waited until he was attacked himself before identifying his enemy, and has always been resolved 'to overthrow all those conditions which make of man a humiliated, enslaved, abandoned and contemptible being.'

'In this war we are fighting against a total lie in the name of a half-truth', Arthur Koestler wrote in 1943. Despite, and unlike, his more supercilious critics, Koestler has always had the rare courage of pronouncing disagreeable truths at the most awkward moment; that is to say when they are most needed. But the half-truth that we were then defending, those relative values of our bourgeois democratic society, was the ally of a total lie: the Soviet Union. Russia helped to win the war and made inevitable the loss of the peace, even of a provisional peace.

We, the scum of the earth, who did not then feel ourselves to be allied with the totalitarian rivals of the Nazis, refuse today to accept the alliance of those other totalitarian rivals of Stalin's. The plague germs of yesterday, conquered but still a very real danger, believe themselves to be justified after the event by the fact that today we are fighting against the cholera germs. They are wrong; our anti-totalitarianism is total, and our memories are inexpungeable.

McCarthyism as a weapon against Communism is ridiculously ineffective, among other reasons because it employs the totalitarian method of 'chain identification' according to which it would be as easy to maintain that the theories of the Monk Mendel were a weapon forged by the Vatican to enable Truman to carry out bacteriological warfare against the proletariat of the world, as to maintain that General Marshall is an agent of Stalin's who sold China to Mao Tse-tung and who would have handed over to him the town of Zenith, Ohio, if the vigilant Babbits had not prevented this. Wherever chain identification is practised, by the Stalinists throughout the world as well as by the McCarthyists, the same phenomena invariably appear; the political police assumes a supernatural ability to blot out the memory of indisputable facts, and the 'logic of the struggle' is invoked, with the result that to attract attention is to be suspected, while suspicion automatically means condemnation; treason becomes loyalty, and loyalty treason.

Chain identification in the United States is restricted in practice and is openly opposed by those men who fight against tyranny wherever it raises its head. But both there, and here in Europe, it is also opposed by those men who are only too enthusiastically in its favour when it is employed exclusively behind the Iron Curtain. The Prague trials among so many others, the accusations levelled against the Jewish doctors which followed and preceded so many other similar accusations raised against the Jews in all the cities of the Soviet Union, for all these horrors and tragedies they have not one drop of ink to spill. But they are prepared to devote tons of newsprint to protests against the 'witchhunt' which never killed a single man. (There is also of course that fashionable anti-Americanism which, as Bebel said of anti-Semitism, is a socialism for imbeciles in addition to being a form of snobbery. Anti-Americanism, anti-Semitism and snobbery are all three based upon a foolish pride in not being that which one is not, and on the false assumption that one is, as a result, that which one also is not.)

No, we do not want the McCarthys and their sort on our side in our struggle against Stalinism, any more than we want the Sartres and their sort on our side in our simultaneous struggle against the McCarthyists.

There does not exist a single truth which we should smother for tactical reasons, nor any form of baseness which we should be prepared to gloss over, even provisionally.

It may be doubted whether the left can continue without drawing sustenance from an eschatological hope, but it is certain that it cannot advance if it does not fight against every form of mystification that it encounters upon its way. That is why its struggle for liberty is always accompanied by a search for truth, a pursuit of knowledge and of consciousness.

The left, and in this it differs from any sort of official left-wing philosophy, has nothing to promise but the struggle, nothing to offer but the search, which accustoms men to live outside, and against, the absolute.

January/February 1953

THE POLICE CONCEPTION OF HISTORY

The Police Conception of History

What total, what totalitarian stupidity! The police don't make history. All they can do is punctuate it, usually wrongly and ungrammatically, during occasional dark ages.

The Liberal régimes have solemn phrases which they trot out when they are celebrating their anniversaries. The others pride themselves on possessing a sacrosanct ideology and pretend to find their justification in a conception of history. But whether this conception be religious, idealistic, heroic or materialistic, in practice it quickly becomes a police conception, in the measure that any solution based on compromise seems to be excluded; for with such a government all real contradiction automatically becomes internal or external conflict.

The following pages—which deal with political trials, with the treason legend, with Sacco and Vanzetti, and with the Rosenberg case—are concerned with this unadmitted police conception, as practised by the governments and demagogues whose aim it is to "denuclearize" the human individual.

A total power can only remain enthroned upon the dead souls of humiliated and broken men. The sort of warfare that it fights, with the object of atomizing men's psyches, is not a novel phenomenon, but thanks to the means available nowadays it is capable, for the first time, of embracing the whole globe.

---

1. Political Trials

Political trials are only a continuation of the political struggle by other means. They allow power to show itself to its subjects in a new and superlative disguise, namely as Justice; whereas the régime's enemies, and with them their cause, are reduced by the appropriate technique to the scale and wretchedness of the individual facing trial, to his errors, and to the faults and fissures in his past. Thus the enemy can be blamed for failing to show that total perfection which is never asked of any man save in the dock. The outcome of the struggle which takes place between the conqueror and his prisoner would be certainly predictable if it were the last that the power had to fight in order to establish its government, its administrative methods, its social system. But a power's last battle is never the one in which it is victorious.

As with crimes of passion, wars and revolutions, political trials are an attempt to resolve an epic conflict by dramatisation. Hence the inevitable artificiality of all such melodramas: Justice now plays the part of a persecuting innocence and takes human life in a frenzy of self-pity, the fury of which can never be quenched. Power is endowed with a permanently clear conscience thanks to the institutions which its laws protect, and can therefore act in its sovereign capacity with the most perfect ill-faith. This is the décor against which the drama is enacted—enacted but never written for its authors cannot claim responsibility for their play: it is essential that it be the result of immaculate conception in the womb of Justice.

In most such dramas we see simultaneously an artificial (or divine) creation of substance, and a sublimation or rarefaction of the consequent realities.

The story of Cain is a good example. Adam's eldest son sacrifices the fruits of the earth to the Supreme Being, while Abel sacrifices the first born of his flock and their fat. Each of them gives that which he has. Now the Supreme Being looks favourably upon Abel and his offering, but averts his eyes from Cain, who is quite understandably offended. And God, instead of consoling him, belabours him with a lecture particularly ill-chosen in view of the circumstances. The Almighty does not deign to waste a single word of explanation concerning His strange attitude, His formidable prejudice. Later we are told that Cain meets Abel in his fields and kills him. What had he said to him? What answer had been offered by God's favourite? What was Abel doing in his brother's fields? In a book by an author who loves to go into a great deal of minute detail far less important than this, not a word of enlightenment is vouchsafed us. Then follows the strange dialogue between the Supreme Being and the murderer: Cain is to be the only man who shall never in any circumstances suffer a violent death. After this happy ending, obscure and thoroughly suspect, one cannot help feeling that God in His professional omniscience, being incapable of making a mistake or of failing to foresee the future, has wished to be rid of Abel. And one fact is worth noticing: the element of provocation is very common in those facts of which political trials are the dramatisation.

Let us take another example: the Socrates affair. Both his accusers and the public knew very well that this was a case of trying the master and friend of Critias, of Charmides and of a great many other enemies of the democratic system. Now the general amnesty pronounced after the fall of the Thirty Tyrants forbade a political accusation, even as Melitos' own past scarcely allowed him to present a brief which insisted on the political content; finally the instigator of the whole business, the redoubtable Anytos, had no wish to parade his long-standing animosity and the persistent jealousy that he had felt for Socrates. For his part the philosopher, and after him his great biographer, a convinced anti-democrat, had no reason to refuse to take part in this deadly masquerade, which was deliberately mounted in order to deprive the trial of its real content.

The accusation that Socrates had introduced new religious practices was ridiculous, but it was perfectly typical of that process of 'transference' which, without hiding the true reasons for the struggle, substitutes mythical shadows in place of the real interests involved. That abhorrence of the void which exists in physical nature corresponds to a horror of the abstract in psychic matters. Such transference serves to incarnate, one might almost say to materialise, the abstract; thanks to it justice, destiny, fertility and so on become divine ladies, the objects of a sensual perception. It is not in order to know whether Jesus was *homo-ousos* or *homoi-ousos*, that is to say quite obviously for an iota, that men were sent to massacre one another, nor for a square of bunting called a flag; men die and murder one another for real interests, but these are sublimated and rarified by a process of transference.

Indeed their pseudonymous nature characterises most political trials: 'Throughout the entire revolution one unchanging method was used by the Robespierrists to kill their enemies: one standard accusation. What was the charge against Jacques Roux? Theft. Against Hébert? Theft. And Fabre? Theft. And Danton? Theft. When Robespierre himself perished he had already begun to deal with Cambon, whom he had accused of "peculation" on the eighth Thermidor.' Thus speaks Michelet.

Since treason is a crime of extreme gravity, why in political trials do the accusers insist on comparatively minor misdemeanours such as theft, prevarication and so on? Why the infamous 'amalgam' in Danton's trial? Why in the Moscow, Budapest and Prague trials was it considered necessary to destroy the revolutionary pasts of the accused, to maintain retroactively that their lives had never been political, and to show them as the auxiliaries of the police, as thieves and swindlers? Or to take examples from another age, why were heretics accused of having been bribed by the Devil's gold, of having in a word committed their spiritual crimes for purposes of mercenary gain?

The answer is that a tyrannical government or church cannot admit that there may be reasons for the existence of an opposition; as a result it must deny that its enemies can be motivated by anything else but vice. They must be loathsome criminals disguised by a trick as a political opposition or as a heterodoxy. They are no longer human beings, but evil beasts; mad dogs, lascivious vipers, disgusting rats. And the purpose of the trials is to snatch from these monsters the human masks behind which they have been hiding.

In a well-staged political trial there is no mention of politics—save in the rhetorical platitudes that roll from the lips of the advocate general. The accused have only one part to play: they must be baseness unmasked, and their political pasts must remain completely invisible.

As for the accused, they have every interest in bringing the political complex fully out into the open and in restoring to the trial its real nature, thus destroying the comedy of Justice. Their courage derives from their conviction that real justice, even if not the law under which they live, is on their side, and from the certainty that they alone represent the future. To be vilified by the government against which they are fighting only serves to reinforce their awareness that they are the servants of a just cause, that they incarnate the honour of their people and of all humanity. A revolutionary in the dock is a prisoner, but he is not a defeated man. The frenzy of his persecutors seems to show him his own strength; even in chains he is causing the men in power to tremble and compelling them to mobilise against him the entire apparatus of their authority. That which the oppressed scarcely dare whisper to one another, he can shout aloud before the entire world. By exploiting the possibilities offered him in this murderous comedy, he can transform it into a tragedy of which he will be the hero; and though he must die in the fifth act, he will do so not as a condemned criminal but as the victim of mystificators who are killing for the sake of inadmissible interests.

Before their judges the *Narodniki* terrorists had no hesitation in accepting full responsibility for their actions, and in loudly pronouncing what their intentions had been and still were. They refused to allow their motives to be hidden in shadow, and despising those subterfuges which might have saved their lives, they attacked. Their trials, even more than the acts of violence that they had perpetrated, caused the Czarist Empire to tremble. They set an example which constantly and everywhere rekindled the faith of other revolutionaries.

'The public prosecutor demands that you arrest me without awaiting judgment because, he says, it is inconceivable that I should not take flight. Mr Prosecutor, I fully believe that you, were you to find yourself in my position, would flee. But a Social Democrat does not do this, for he accepts the responsibility of his actions. And now, gentlemen of the bench, condemn me!' Such were the words which Rosa Luxemburg addressed to the Frankfurt Tribunal, and it did indeed find her guilty of demoralising the army. Four and a half years later the revolution secured her release from prison; within a few weeks the counter-revolutionaries had assassinated her—secretly, without trial, just as Matteotti was executed in Italy and Trotsky was murdered by an agent of Stalin's in Mexico.

The totalitarian régimes, during a period of global wars, need their political trials; they have perfected the stage sets down to the smallest details. Those of their enemies incapable of playing the part assigned them in this ceremonial theatre are punished without trial. Entire nations are now living beneath the shadow of these trials which they are compelled to applaud with cries of: 'Shoot them, hang them!' A religion is born, and its gospel is the legend of treason.

---

2. The Legend of Treason

High treason—which in many penal codes is defined as a plot against the security of the state—is the only crime for which there is punishment in the case of failure and honour in success. Successful treason is an act of loyalty all the more courageous because it is loyalty-by-foresight, while failure simply serves to underline the felony.

The word treason is obviously meaningless if it is not used within a frame of reference that also contains the concept of loyalty. We are not betrayed by our enemies. Ulysses deceived the Trojans, but he did not betray them.

A monarchy is based upon the love and loyalty that the subjects owe to their monarch. Whoever commits by word or deed the crime of lèse-majesté is therefore betraying his monarch, just as a husband who sleeps with any woman other than his wife is an adulterer in a monogamous society. Such simple relations do not exist in modern states. To be opposed to the government is not illicit, for it is not the government that claims a citizen's loyalty and love but the country, the nation of which the government represents the provisionary will without in consequence being identified therewith. Nevertheless a government desirous of being strong is always tempted to treat any opposition it meets as though that opposition were hostility directed against the nation itself, as though it were in fact treacherous. This tendency becomes dominant in times of war or when the nation is split asunder by acute internal strife. The opposition is then denounced as working for the foreign enemy, by means of a *chain identification:* it weakens the government, hence the state, hence the country. Therefore it is in the service of the enemy. It knows this. Why does it act as it is doing? Because it is the enemy's agent. It is not traitorous because it is opposed to the government, but it is in opposition because it is treacherous. Once this point has been established, everything becomes as simple as the working of a guillotine. It is now proved beyond dispute that the government is the entire nation.

Did the Devil not exist, God would be soon snowed under by the rebuffs that He suffers daily. Did treason not exist, an absolute government would be unable to maintain its pretence of perfection. In both cases it is a question of dissociating the inseparable; a single and total power must disclaim all responsibility for anything that is not a glorious success. If Moscow is starving, the answer is to shoot a few score workmen who are betraying their country in the interest of whomsoever has been selected as the enemy of the day; it is thus proved that Moscow, thanks to an infallible government plan, would have been well fed had it not been for sabotage. The people can well do without meat or butter or eggs for a few weeks; the government cannot do without treason for so much as a single day.

There are probably human beings who really have no conception of what is meant by paternal love, joy, sympathy, friendship; but there is probably not one man who has not at least once—usually between the ages of three and five—experienced the feeling that he has been betrayed by precisely that person whom he has hitherto believed loved him most. This experience, misunderstood and quickly divorced from the real event, almost always passes into the unconscious; it remains, in effect, the basis for the truly astonishing credulity with which all men everywhere accept the legend of treason. This credulity is reinforced from many sources: soldiers fleeing from the battle have only to believe themselves betrayed in order no longer to regard themselves as cowards. Thus the conviction of being betrayed is, like the idea of suicide, a negative comfort which permits the individual as well as the group to avoid awareness of its own faults, errors and weaknesses. Hitler was the perfect example of the betrayed man. He began his political career with the certainty that the 1918 Revolution had caused, and not followed, the defeat of the German Army; he committed suicide convinced that his people, unworthy of its Führer, had betrayed him.

Treason is an immense legend spread about the globe, existing both in public and private lives; over and above that, it is a reality. But how important is the reality? It seems highly probable that in those battles in which small tribes fought for their lives, an act of treason could be decisive; it is certain that the destiny of no nation has ever been determined by treachery. Athens did not lose the Peloponnesian War because of Alcibiades' desertion, despite the serious consequences of the strategic advice which he gave to the Spartans and from which they knew how to profit. Later, confronted by Philip, even if every Athenian had been on the side of Demosthenes, Athens would never have been in a position to defeat an army capable of conquering whole continents. Philip of Macedon's gold did not buy him his victories; it did buy him a public opinion which feared the hardships of war and preferred defeat without fighting. The Athenians of that epoch, when searching for their own greatness, looked towards the past and not to the future.

Espionage, as old as the history of the world, has assumed a new importance in modern mythology. The spy makes as good a movie hero as the great gangster or the skilled detective: when serving your country or your cause he is the most sublime of beings; when he works for the enemy, the most ignoble of criminals. If battles took place according to a pre-arranged plan, spying would be a most useful undertaking. But that is not the case. Any secret can be stolen save that of a future which no man knows. Long before 1914 the Schlieffen Plan was known to the French, having been handed over by a German officer; but this made no difference to the course of events. As it happened, the

Germans abandoned that plan at the decisive moment. In the Good Old Days the buying of victories, of the enemy's field marshals either with or without their troops, was often only a matter of finding the money. Louis XIV did extremely good business in the enemy's headquarter camps. Just so long as his armies were the stronger, the better equipped, and were regularly paid, he could win almost every victory. But the sum total of his victories and conquests was not even worth the price of corruption: let alone the price of blood.

A man who would attempt to explain history in terms of various acts of treason would obviously have no trouble in finding traitors at work almost everywhere, but his researches would deprive him of the ability to recognise the truly determinant factors in the evolution of humanity. No empire, no government, no nation has perished as the result of treason, but treason has always been present during their decline: treason is in fact a symptom of decline. It has undoubtedly been of service to future conquerors, but its greatest misdeed has been to hide from the moribund the threat which they carried within themselves like a secret illness. Revolutions have never liquidated any but dying régimes, systems adapted to a past which each day was growing more and more irrelevant.

Secrecy is one of the indispensable characteristics of all treason. Now, if conspiracy has frequently proved successful inside a régime, when it was a question simply of replacing one tyrant by another or one oligarchy by its rival, it has yet never succeeded in overthrowing a social order. On the contrary, every revolution has been openly announced, every decline has been preceded by countless warnings. In April of 1917 Lenin publicly opposed the Central Committee of his Party and issued Trotsky's order of the day: 'All power to the Soviets!' The only conspiracy which he controlled was directed against the other left wing parties within the Soviets, but apart from certain executive details, which in any event were denounced by Gorki, there was nothing secret about the action which resulted in his seizure of power. Hitler never attempted to conceal the fact that he had made up his mind to destroy the Weimar Republic. There was nothing esoteric about the Nazi bible, *Mein Kampf*. It gave a complete programme of what he planned to do.

In this epoch of revolutions and counter-revolutions, successful *putsches* are only either the openings of civil wars or the theatrical apotheosis of victory won without fighting: for example, Mussolini's March on Rome or Gottwald's seizure of power in Prague. Those revolutions which shatter and destroy conquered empires at the end of total wars have nothing whatever in common with a *coup d'état* prepared and carried out by conspirators.

Since the totalitarian régime came into existence, the treason legend has become a far more important political phenomen than treason itself. The Communist régime as fashioned by Stalin has used this legend as the most solid basis on which to build what continues to be called its "ideology", its "dialectic" etc. In order that every subject may be a potential traitor, laws are passed declaring as secrets of state anything that any spy might ever see; the number of pairs of socks knitted in such and such a factory of Eastern Germany, the degree of enthusiasm shown by a group of young Communists in some Moravian village, the result of the potato harvest in the Minsk district—everything! By simultaneously proclaiming that it is every citizen's sacred duty to denounce spies, and by treating as traitor any man who refuses to do this, the state demands that every citizen shall show his loyalty in the sole convincing manner: by betraying his fellows. After Stalinisation, the Communist parties are integrated into this system which only recognises loyalty in unconditional submission and in the betrayal of anything which in any circumstances might be regarded as opposition to the government of the U.S.S.R.

Behind the Iron Curtain the peoples have no choice but to submit to this system, though they despise its violent hypocrisy and fear the perpetual threat that it entails; but in the non-Communist countries, the Stalinists have chosen it quite freely, making of it their moral and intellectual guide. Though in their private lives their standard of honesty may be high, politically they think and act solely according to this sort of double-book-keeping, which enables them to betray with perfectly clear consciences, and permits them to condemn all those who do not espouse their cause as ignoble traitors. It is from this point of view that the attitude of the Rosenbergs, from the beginning of the affair until its atrocious ending, must be considered as the typical result of that Stalinisation of men who joined a movement in order to act as revolutionaries, and who, in order to remain within it, accepted that they be transformed into agents; agents willing to submit unconditionally and ready to deny even themselves, to deny even the sense of their ultimate sacrifice.

Inconceivable ignorance persists among those who were rightly opposed to the execution of the Rosenbergs, and there is a stubborn ignorance among those who, apart from Communist Party members, proclaimed the couple's innocence. It is only such gross ignorance which has made possible the comparison of this affair with that of Sacco and Vanzetti.

It is right that human conscience should rebel against any injustice which it sees being enacted on our planet. But is also right that those who protest should be neither too lazy nor too cowardly to attempt to discover the reality. Ignorance is not one of man's imprescriptible rights.

---

3.   Sacco and Vanzetti

They were two Italian anarchists. Nicola Sacco worked in a boot factory; Bartolomeo Vanzetti was a labourer, builder and hawker of fish. The accusation against them was that at Bridgewater, Massachusetts, they had attacked the accountant of a factory who was transporting $ 16,000 on his person, had robbed him, and had killed both him and another man who was with him as body-guard. In open court there was no mention of anything save this vulgar crime; but behind the scenes, in the official campaign intended to decide the attitude of the jury and affect the opinion of influential men, all was politics, beginning with the secret dossiers compiled by the political police which were not shown to the defence until the very end of the case. During seven long years, while the two condemned men awaited execution, the whole elaborate edifice built by the police slowly collapsed: it was shown how men had been recruited to give false evidence, while the real witnesses, those who had seen something but who refused to yield to police pressure, were systematically kept away from the court. Finally one member of the gang which had actually committed the Bridgewater crime confessed. There was every reason to hope that Sacco and Vanzetti must now be set free. But from the very beginning Barto had said to his friends: 'There is nothing to be done, they will kill us. We must fight against them of course, and I shall continue the struggle for the rest of my life, henceforth in far better conditions than ever before, because the number of those listening to us will be so much greater—but they will kill us.'

He announced to the judges: 'I have fought all my life for the elimination of all crimes, including the crime that is consecrated and sanctified by law: the crime which is the exploitation and the oppression of one man by another. And that is why I am here, that is why you are condemning me: you are making me suffer because I am a revolutionary, and you may be quite sure that I am one indeed. My convictions are so strong that even if you could execute me twice over, and I could yet come back to life, I would do again everything that I have done before.'

The impresarios who mounted this judicial spectacle had chosen these two *wops* because they were known as persistent anarchist agitators, but also because they were simple working men whose English was so poor that they would be bound to need an interpreter in court. (They were given one: the man was a friend of the judge, Webster Thayer, who, from the very beginning of the trial, promised all right-thinking men that he would have these two anarchists grilled on the electric chair.) Furthermore Vanzetti and Sacco appeared to be isolated; they were against every sort of organisation, every political party, against the unions—they believed only in a free community of men inspired by the same ideas, fighting for the same ideals and linked by a fraternal solidarity. (In 1938 Alexander Weissberg met an anarchist of this same sort in the G.P.U. prison called the Brekhalovka. He was a little Jewish tailor named Aizenberg who openly proclaimed his convictions. This man underwent a 'conveyer interrogation', that is to say uninterrupted questioning lasting for thirty-one days and thirty-one nights, and he was the only man so tortured who did not give in. The author of *The Accused* ends his description of this extraordinary episode thus: 'There was no way of dealing with him ... Of the twelve thousand prisoners he was the only one who was fighting for an idea. We others were the victims of oppression, while he was fighting against oppression.')

The most serious of the many mistakes committed by the policemen and by the judicial apparatus was undoubtedly concerned with the personality of Barto Vanzetti. He had the face of a Byronic lover, the figure of a Don Quixote, the soul of a prophet and the energy of an apostle—a lay saint who did not desire martyrdom but who was prepared to undergo it. During the last seven years of his life, lived upon the very threshold of death, he far surpassed anything that might have been expected of such a man. He read enormously, he wrote, even in English, a language that he had learned in prison. This man in chains became the most free being in the world, a conscience with all the universe for its domain. 'If none of this had happened, I should have passed my life making speeches to people at street corners, trying to sow the seeds of rebellion among them. I should have died in obscurity and been forgotten after a wasted life ... Without this accident, we should never have been able to do so much for justice, for tolerance, and for mutual understanding among men.'

These two victims became towers of strength, owing nothing to anybody and everything to their conscience. No political party has been able to claim their heritage, and their case has refused every sort of transference. 'My name will mean justice and liberty, nothing else', Vanzetti predicted. The Communists were unable to exploit their corpses—those two anarchists hated the police and military régime of the Soviet Union.

Later the anti-Fascists were to follow the road that Sacco and Vanzetti had marked out. They had shown how to strip provocation naked, how to refuse that a political trial be deprived of its political element, how to make all transference impossible. Since that night of August 22nd, 1927, revolutionaries have known that it is possible 'to triumph in agony'.

Bartolomeo Vanzetti was already strapped to the electric chair when he said: 'I still wish to forgive those few men who are doing this to me.' Nicola Sacco's last words were: '*Viva l'Anarchia!*'

---

4. The Rosenberg Case

Sacco and Vanzetti died the victims of a trial to which they had attempted throughout seven years to give its true political significance: namely, the class struggle. The Rosenbergs died after a trial and an immense publicity campaign from which both they and their defenders had systematically removed all political meaning, blotting out the very content of their social life and those factors which had decided both their unadmitted acts and also the attitude in which they persisted until they were executed.

The self-assurance of today's ideologists is largely based upon the fact that they are, perhaps deliberately, out of date. Specifically they are out of date by one war, one hidden counter-revolution, one totalitarianism, one resistance and countless revolts against injustice. It is therefore necessary to dissipate certain misunderstandings concerning the meaning of innocence.

When Captain Dreyfus proclaimed his innocence, he was in perfect agreement with his judges and with the law in condemning the crime of which he was accused: he was convinced that there was no valid excuse for so evil a deed, no alternative interpretation which, for example, would allow a Frenchman to decide according to his political views whether or not he was right to deliver a secret of state to another country.

The most detailed examination of his character, of his beliefs, of his family's situation and of his financial status does not allow us to discover the slightest motive for a crime which he himself would have regarded as bringing down total and permanent dishonour upon his head. A definite contradiction between the man and the act of which he is accused does not prove his innocence in crimes of passion, but is a decisive argument when it is a question of logical crimes, of a sustained and organised course of action.

Sacco and Vanzetti were certainly not opposed to political violence nor to the expropriation of the capitalists, but they were the sworn enemies of vulgar misdemeanours such as theft. They would have felt themselves thereby to be dishonoured forever, and that is why they rejected as an ignominious attack upon their cause the accusation which attempted to transform a political charge, to which their accusers dare not admit, into a vulgar criminal offence.

The deeds of which the Rosenbergs were accused are considered by every Communist in the world not as a crime but as a duty carried out towards the Socialist Fatherland, all the more meritorious in the very measure by which they expose their authors to the rigours of capitalist law. Acts of treason—towards whom? Just so long as Klaus Fuchs felt himself to be a Communist, he obviously regarded the transmission of atomic secrets to agents of the U.S.S.R. as a proof of his loyalty. When he broke with Stalinism and confessed to what he had done, he immediately became a traitor in the eyes of every Communist. In his own eyes Fuchs was innocent, though a traitor, just so long as he remained integrated into the system of Communist loyalties, which freed him of the duty of being either loyal or sincere in his attitude towards the non-Communist world. It is easy to understand that the Rosenbergs can have regarded themselves as innocent until the very end of their lives; the publicity campaign on their behalf must have confirmed them in this belief.

During the war Julius Rosenberg was a civilian employee working for a branch of the army, the Newark Signal Corps. He ceased work in February of 1945 and was finally dismissed because it had been discovered that he was a secret member of the Communist Party, specifically that he had been a member of Branch 16B of the 'Industrial Division' of the Communist Party until February of 1944, when he was transferred to the 'Eastern Club of the First Assembly District' with number 12179. Rosenberg denied most energetically that he was a Communist and he approached congressmen and other influential persons to intervene on his behalf. He signed a declaration on oath: 'I am not now and I have never been a Communist sympathiser... The charge against me is based upon a confusion of identities or upon a complete falsehood. In any event it has no basis in fact' (page 1185).[1] When asked during the course of the trial to state whether this declaration was true or not, he refused to reply, invoking the Fifth Amendment which allows any witness to refuse to answer any question that might incriminate himself. This refusal to answer, which the jury interpreted as being if not a proof of guilt at least one of ill-faith, had a disastrous effect, but doubtless less disastrous than the preliminary interrogation of Ethel Rosenberg. In her testimony she maintained that both she and her husband were completely innocent, and categorically denied all the facts upon which the accusation against them was based. Now seven months before, between 7th and 11th August, 1950, she had appeared as a witness *sub poena* before a Grand Jury and had there systematically refused to answer questions concerning these same facts, claiming protection of the Fifth Amendment. Is it possible to imagine the wife of Captain Dreyfus refusing to answer the following questions: did, or did not, her husband have relationships with the German Espionage Service, did he belong to a Pan-German organisation, etc? It is not hard to understand that the Grand Jury was astonished by this witness's attitude. One of the few facts to which she did admit was that she had consulted her lawyer, Emmanuel Bloch. The jurymen thought that Ethel Rosenberg might have misunderstood the legal advice he had given her, but since she persisted in this same attitude during her second interrogation by the Grand Jury, which took place four days later, such an explanation was obviously invalid. Thus when she faced trial the state prosecutor had only to quote the evidence that she had given before the Grand Jury (pages 1349 to 1402) in order to destroy any credibility that might have been attached to

---

[1] The quotations with page numbers are taken from *The Transcript of Record—Supreme Court of the United States*, October Term 1951, Nos. 111 and 112. The second volume contains the records of appeals and of the decisions taken by higher authorities.

what Ethel Rosenberg now said. Her proclamation of innocence coming after this quite inexplicable delay appeared grossly insincere. Another important point that arose in her interrogation by the Grand Jury was the question of finding out whether she had ever met Harry Gold. To this question the wife of Julius Rosenberg replied: 'I refuse to answer for the reason that this might intimidate, I mean incriminate me' (page 1386). A pitiful and mechanical performance, in which this slip of the tongue is the only clue to character. It is known that it was Gold's confession which led to the discovery of the activities of Greenglass and the Rosenbergs.

What is new in the trial of the Rosenbergs is that we here encounter for the first time a state of affairs in which it is the accused, and not their accusers, who are determined to eliminate the political content. It is true that we have already seen a similar attitude adopted elsewhere, though in very different conditions: in the Moscow trials, in those of Prague, Budapest and so on. There the accused never attempted to explain the reasons for their opposition to the régime. Bukharin, for example, did not say: 'Yes, I exposed at the proper time the criminal errors of Stalinist collectivisation, I correctly predicted that it would ruin our agricultural wealth and would destroy the productive force of millions of men liquidated for no purpose.' But the Rosenbergs were in New York. Even there they were obedient to the same master's voice that had prompted the Moscow accused, to the same totalitarian police. The same rule of depersonalisation and of depolitisation, in the same shadow game, turned the Rosenbergs into harmless little bourgeois figures, innocent of everything, even though they had committed the crime; while on the far side of the Iron Curtain that rule makes the victims of the M.V.D. absolute criminals, meet to be punished for crimes that never were committed. Rosenberg might have said: 'I love my country, that is why I wish to see it become a Soviet republic and conquer the future. Meanwhile I am giving all that is best in me to the service of the U.S.S.R., the Socialist Fatherland of us all, whose defence is the supreme duty of those who would ensure the happiness of mankind. I am a revolutionary and I am fighting for a cause which is equally that of the Americans and of the Russians. In helping the U.S.S.R. I have not committed a crime of espionage on behalf of a foreign power; at the risk of my life I have been attempting to increase the military strength of a state which will liberate us one day, as it has already liberated eight hundred millions of men upon our globe. I and my family have lived a simple and hardworking life. You will discover no base motive for what I have done nor for what you accuse me of having done. I shall know how to die, if need be, for my convictions.'

If Rosenberg, misled but faithful to one revolutionary tradition, had spoken in such terms, the Party would have declared him a traitor, an *agent provocateur*, a Fascist, and there would have been not the slightest publicity campaign on his behalf.

During the trial and for a short time after its conclusion, the 'apparatus' undertook no action on behalf of the Rosenbergs. It was not yet sure that the couple would maintain the line of conduct, that they would not weaken and put their affairs in other hands than those of Mr Bloch. Only when the Communists were quite reassured on this point did they launch their campaign, but to begin with they took the line that this was a Jewish matter, presenting the couple as the victims of anti-Semitism. In this case this was a particularly difficult transference, but it promised results, for the obedient Rosenbergs accepted the novel rôle and behaved and spoke as though they were traditional Jews, even practising ones. As a result, those of their letters which were destined for the public reflected an entirely fictitious frame of mind. This line had to be abandoned, however, when anti-Semitism behind the Iron Curtain became too virulent; the campaign on their behalf had to change its nature once again. Even while the Slansky trial was going on in Prague and the Jewish doctors were being arrested in Moscow—to which of course the accused couple never once referred—Julius Rosenberg could speak, on 23rd November, 1953, of 'a campaign of hatred fomented to associate in people's minds Communism with anti-Semitism.' On the 6th of May, 1952, however, Ethel Rosenberg had sent her best wishes to the newly created state of Israel, remarking that its birthday, May 14th, was the same as that of her younger son. Yet when the Communists launched their campaign of hatred against Israel there is not one word of surprise or of protest in the Rosenbergs' letters.

The introduction and the commentaries on these letters, in the French edition, are not signed. The author is as insincere as are the letters, when they are not expressing conjugal or family sentiments. Ethel Rosenberg wrote on the 21st of June, 1951: 'I feel so discouraged by this injustifiable attack against a legally constituted American party! The spectre of Fascism is beginning to emerge, huge and menacing; the concentration camps are being made ready.' What party is she talking about, what is this unjustified attack? The commentary explains: 'Seventeen men and women had been arrested and accused in New York under the Smith Act, recently passed.' The commentator does not say that these were officials of the Communist Party, and it does not tell the reader very much about the Smith Act: it omits to mention that during the war the Communists had aroused American opinion in an attempt to have a group of Trotskyists condemned precisely under this extremely doubtful Smith Act. On the 4th of July, 1951, Rosenberg wrote: 'I have cut the text of the Declaration of Independence out of the *New York Times*. It is interesting to read, in these circumstances, what it has to say about freedom of speech, freedom of the press and freedom of religion.' He may have cut out that text, but he had certainly not read it; he had not read those words about freedom of this or that, for the good reason that they are not in the Declaration . . . Later, on May 24th, 1953, he was to say with considerable truth: 'When there is no longer freedom of expression, there is no longer freedom of conscience.' That remark is directed against his own country, where his letters were being published in the newspapers and in pamphlets, where propaganda was being openly made on behalf of the Rosenbergs, directed exclusively against the 'free' world— the quotation marks are Rosenberg's—and not against the countries of Slansky and of Beria.

The editor says: 'The letters contained in this book have been selected from among several hundred . . . They do not deal with the facts concerning the affair.' Why not? But in any case this statement is untrue. The letters written before the verdict was pronounced (between 25th July, 1950, and 14th November, 1950) are indeed silent about the case; they conform fully with the rôle that the accused couple proposed to play in court: a simple family, never involved in matters that did not concern it, with the sole ambition of continuing to live 'an honest and constructive' life. But once sentence has been pronounced, the tenor of this correspondence changes. The letters are to be published and this the writers know. They are increasingly aware that they are located at the centre of a political action—but then how are they to play their rôle in this, having constantly refused to treat the case as a political one? Thus everything remains in a state of artificial *chiaroscuro*, to the very end, which is certainly tragic: as tragic as the two persons' death was real. On October 18th, 1951, Ethel Rosenberg wrote: 'Nevertheless, despite all the unhappiness and torment, nothing can shake my belief that only the pure and noble are enabled to find themselves on this thorny road!' Her husband echoes this sentiment: 'We shall continue to hold fast with all the progressives, for the sake of honesty, liberty, peace and true justice.' And later: '. . . We have, I believe, given eloquent expression to the greatest and unique aspiration of humanity.' What is he talking about? They are, he declares, absolutely innocent, they have been subjected to no sort of torture nor even maltreatment during the interrogation, during the trial or later. What, then, is this struggle in which they are engaged; for what 'most noble interests' for what 'greatest and unique aspiration of humanity' have they been working? When? How? 'We have never wavered, we have shown ourselves worthy of the task assigned to us,' Rosenberg wrote on October 18th, 1951. What task? Was it the task of opposing those who suggest 'to the people the idea that the followers of a certain political philosophy are inclined to espionage?' If so the Rosenbergs certainly failed to carry out their task. Instead of hiding behind the Fifth Amendment, they should have announced proudly: 'Yes, we are Communists, and you have involved us in the affair of the spy Greenglass in order to spread the idea that Communists are spies. Now we, the Communists on trial here, are innocent, while

Greenglass, who is a spy, is not a Communist!' But the Party did not allow them to speak such words.

These letters, when they do not reflect the love between a man, his wife and their children, display a methodical insincerity or an extreme and sincere hypocrisy, a hypocrisy of a schizoid nature which is the genuine product of a Stalinist education.

In a letter to her lawyer, Ethel Rosenberg describes a visit of her mother's, and writes that she is 'still stupefied by the amoral impudence' of the old woman who had advised her to confirm the evidence given by Greenglass. It is in fact known that the mother had no illusions about her son, and was convinced that only her elder daughter could have dragged young David into a course of action which would have such terrible results. Only Ethel Rosenberg could have done this, for she alone had sufficient authority over her younger brother, and of all those with whom he was linked, she and her husband were the only active members of the Communist Party.

The most extraordinary explanations have been given, apparently based on moral considerations, for Greenglass's attitude. Nevertheless there is no enigma, no moral problem; just as Harry Gold had to confess once Klaus Fuchs had given the authorities all the facts, so Greenglass had no choice but to admit that he had transmitted secret information to Gold. On the other hand he could have refused to answer the question as to who had recruited him for the work in which Gold was the contact man. The police would doubtless have ended by suspecting the Rosenbergs, but would have been unable to prove that they were accomplices. What reason did Greenglass have for making his complete admissions? One and one alone: to secure the safety of his wife, who was as deeply compromised in this business as was he. The price he had to pay for this was not that he denounce the Rosenbergs, but that he denounce those people by whom and through whom he was linked to the Soviet Secret Service. The young man preferred to save the wife whom he loved rather than his sister and his brother-in-law whom he had venerated in his youth but who he now felt had victimised him. He, the only proletarian member of this family, and it may be remarked the only working man among all the accused in all these American trials, had only become a Communist as a result of the influence of his elder sister. To tell the truth and therefore to be considered as a traitor by the Party—that is to say by the friends of his elder sister—seemed to him a small matter in comparison with the peril from which he was determined to shield his wife. That he should have acted as he did because he hated the Rosenbergs is an invention of the campaign that was launched after the trial was over. The Rosenbergs were careful not to create this impression, and they had their reasons. The defence counsel attempted to make the jury believe that Greenglass had approached Rosenberg precisely in order that Rosenberg might help him carry out his projected flight, and Julius Rosenberg was thus compelled to give explanations for certain of his actions which he could not deny, notably the fact that he had gone to a doctor and asked for a false medical certificate for Greenglass.

Any man who reads the 1,715 pages of the court record carefully has no alternative but to believe that the Rosenbergs were guilty beyond any reasonable doubt, and in consequence that the unanimous verdict of the twelve jurymen, chosen with the approval of the defence, was a just verdict. What is a striking injustice is the condemnation to death of these people, a verdict pronounced by a judge who had fully deserved the compliment that Mr Bloch paid him on the part of the defence: 'You have treated us with the greatest courtesy and have granted us all those facilities which we could claim as lawyers ... You have presided over this trial with the dignity that is becoming to an American court' (pages 1452 to 1453).

Before pronouncing his terrible sentence, the judge, Irving R. Kaufman, recognized that it was, 'the love of their cause which dominated the life of the Rosenbergs, who as a result placed their devotion to that cause above their personal safety and even above their love for their children.' There cannot be a moment's doubt that he was speaking the truth when he went on to say: 'I have considered this matter for days and nights, and every nerve and fibre of my body has been under stress. I am convinced beyond the shadow of a doubt that you are guilty' (page 1616). Nevertheless this judge committed a fatal error in condemning the Rosenbergs to capital punishment, for he was acting in the spirit of 1951 when contemplating acts committed seven years before and in very different circumstances, circumstances which in effect were then quite the opposite of what they later became. He judged the facts before him in the artificial light, the blinding light of the legend of treason.

In addition to the facts, characters and relationships involved, every political trial reflects public opinion. This trial showed the degradation of the Communists by their own Party, and simultaneously revealed the clash of two treason legends; face to face with the totalitarian legend of the Stalinists, provoked and nourished by it, there emerges here another legend, that by which the American people is trying to explain and excuse the errors of a past for which it is alone and entirely responsible. We see here the encounter of a systematically lying conscience with a conscience dangerously falsified.

'I wished to eliminate the political from this trial and, thanks to the judge, we have been able to eliminate it' (page 1605). Who spoke thus a few days after the verdict and immediately before sentence was pronounced? The prosecution? No, Emmanuel H. Bloch, the Rosenbergs defence counsel. This extremely competent and remarkably skilful lawyer had, from the very beginning of the affair, decided what the attitude of the accused was to be: they behaved exactly according to the rules laid down by the Communist Party for all its members when interrogated by Congressional Commissions of Enquiry. In such circumstances, to hide behind the Fifth Amendment may cost a man his job if he is a public servant. When Emmanuel Bloch perceived that these same tactics, when used in court, might well cost his clients their lives, it was too late, far too late for the defence finally to turn the trial into a political one. For many, many years the G.P.U. had succeeded in killing Communists after having first compelled them to accept an infamous political anonymity; here in New York it succeeded in clothing two beings who were to die on its behalf in a similar anonymity. This deception only worked on those who were determined to be deceived.

But America, having at last entered upon a phase of extreme distrust, was no longer prepared to be abused in this fashion. America was frightened, exaggeratedly so. For the tactics of persons such as the Rosenbergs and the McCarthyite demagogues produce the same effect upon public opinion; they prepare the way in men's minds for the acceptance of the police conception of history, as if it were a message of salvation.

December 1953

ON HATRED

On Hatred *1*

Love is garrulous, forever proclaiming its existence, flaunting itself in song, poems, novels, films, on every Hertzian wavelength; its cries, exploited commercially, are spread across the world with even more insistence than that 'anger of the imbeciles' against which Georges Bernanos railed. Being its own justification, love looks for no reason save when it is threatened by adversity or by that which devalues daily happiness: habit. Happy love ignores its reasons until the moment when, in order to maintain itself alive, it begins to devour them; and that is the death of passion.

As for hatred, it only admits its existence in a flood of argument. It wishes to be regarded not as a feeling, but as a conviction founded upon an undeniable experience. According to the age, it claims to be based on magic, on religion, on philosophy or on science, and over and above that, it maintains that it derives from a sturdy commonsense which even the vilest subterfuges of its enemies cannot undermine.

Unlike love, hatred does not consume the cause of its existence; its actions, and the reactions of others that these inevitably entail, have the contrary effect of increasing its cause day by day. Far from weakening it, habit strengthens and nourishes hatred. The hated man can do nothing that will not make him more hateful yet; even as those whom a paranoiac believes to be his enemies can undertake nothing that will not serve to augment his suspicions of them.

A man or woman who is loved often possesses the power to destroy the passion of which he or she is the object; a hated being can do nothing, or almost nothing, against hatred. He cannot always even be sure that he will blot it out by destroying himself. Hatred is self-sufficient; it would constitute the most tightly sealed form of solitude, if the hater were able to free himself of the intense hostile intimacy that links him with his victim, or the figure he imagines that victim to be. It is incidentally this intimacy which has misled certain psychologists into thinking that hatred should be treated as a form of love, either turned inside out or ill-repaid. Thus have they been led to confuse common dislikes, born of jealousy or envy or of the desire to right a wrong, with true and total hatred, which is a far rarer phenomenon. It is hardly to be encountered in novels, for example, or, when it is, it is usually incarnate in minor characters. A writer soon realises that this maniacal obsession is only in appearance a fruitful theme, and that in reality, owing to its utter sterility, it merely offers material for an anecdote. Even a brilliant satire based solely on hatred would soon peter out, as quickly as would a tragedy in which pity, lacking love, were absent.

During the First World War the propagandists of the belligerent powers stirred up national hatreds intended to approach the intensity of frenzies. Their success did not last, and was almost always nil with the actual combatants, who were killing and dying without hatred and without 'trying to understand'. Similarly, of all the arguments used by a propaganda based on social antagonism, that which should derive its sustenance from the 'class hatred' inherent in the proletariat has been shown to be the weakest.

Functional hatred soon fades away if it is not forcibly fed. Those in whom it has been induced would sooner forget it absolutely. According to historical circumstances, a purely functional hatred and a limitless distrust have alternated with a confidence and a mutual admiration as the basic emotional relationship between Englishmen and Frenchmen. Nevertheless, awareness of the difference between the two nations has remained unchanged, and factors quite independent of the individual will have altered a climate of opinion which changes easily from *allophilia* to *allophobia* or, in less dramatic circumstances, from a sympathetic indifference to a hostile indifference. In either case the "other" against whom these emotions are directed remains truly unknown.

One hatred has existed for thousands of years. It is that which, in the course of the last century, acquired the name of anti-Semitism. An endemic phenomenon, it has on occasion passed through epidemic phases. It then achieves murderous paroxysms, and the very excesses of these seem to weaken it for a time. Its successes, inscribed in the martyrology of the Jewish people as in the history of the nations, have been immense. Its failures, on the other hand, have been even more striking: the people it would persecute and destroy, and which it has attempted throughout so many centuries to blot out, are the only nation of antiquity to have survived into our own age without losing their identity in the process. They alone have arisen again and again without ever denying their own selves. It is true that the Jews numbered approximately five millions at the beginning of the Christian era, and that their numbers have scarcely more than doubled since. This can only be explained by reason of the almost continual loss of life, though these exterminations have never been as total as hatred would have wished. There is no argument which hatred has not found and used in this long campaign; it spoke in the name of a God, whose death it pretended to avenge; in the name, now of emperors, now of slaves; it was the defender of the rich one day, the protector of the poor the next; it advanced as arguments the joy of living and the duty of asceticism; it invoked religious faith and atheism; it claimed as its allies feudalism, capitalism, socialism, communism, racial purity, peace and war. It used every process of vilification and of humiliation, it perfected all the techniques of slander. It killed Jews wherever it could.

Has not this hatred endured precisely because of its thousand year failure, and not despite this? Is it to be concluded that the people which it has persecuted with such a terrifying constancy has managed to remain alive precisely because of this hatred? Because it has never allowed that people a respite long enough to enable the conscience of Israel and its determination to preserve its own existence to weaken, perhaps to vanish...? In the world where hatred reigns, the certainty that the shadow always follows the substance no longer applies. The fear of the persecuted can increase or disappear according to the extent of the danger that threatens them; the anguish of the persecutors, on the other hand, usually remains incurable.

2

To begin with, the name given to hatred of the Jews is a false name. The number of real anti-Semites is minute. They consist of a few intellectuals, mostly Hellenists or Hinduists, who regard certain semitic elements in Christianity as being inferior, and who prefer to them other elements derived from purely pagan sources. In this sense, but not at all in the current sense of the word, Renan, for example, was an anti-Semite. As for the Nazis, they were anxious to forge an alliance with the purest of Semites, the Arabs. They received the Grand Mufti of Jerusalem in Germany as an honoured guest, and took him to Auschwitz to show him how skilfully they were exterminating the Jews. Many anti-Semites today are to be seen in the pro-Arab camp.

The theorists and the most frantic adepts of anti-Semitism are to be found in those nations which accept the Jewish god while refusing His Law, which they replace by pagan traditions of which they have changed the name more than they have altered the content. It is true that F. Lovsky, in his remarkable essay *Antisémitisme et Mystère d'Israel*,[1] insists that there existed a form of anti-Judaism which was expressed in words and deeds long before the Christian era. The Protestant author sees in this fact an additional proof of the existence of that mystery of Israel which inspires in him a love of the Jews, and in the anti-Semites a hatred. Nevertheless he appears to accept the argument of Jules Isaac, who detects in Christian anti-Semitism (and not in the anti-Judaism of antiquity) a frantic desire to dishonour and vilify its victims.

Léon Poliakov is inclined to think that the hostility directed against Israel in various pre-Christian epochs is scarcely different in its nature from that which is normally directed against foreign peoples: 'Rivalries have existed always and everywhere between clans, tribes and peoples. As for ancient Israel, it would be quite vain to try and establish by means of the traditional documents at our disposal, whether or not the hostility directed against that

[1] Published by Albin Michel.

people by its neighbours during the biblical epoch was of a special nature, whether there were any particular virulence in it.'[1] Poliakov, it is true, does not fail to recognise that the, at least relative, isolation resulting from the practice of the Law can, in certain conditions, contribute to those misunderstandings which anti-Semitism spreads abroad and exploits with an indefatigable zeal. Nevertheless the author of the *Histoire de l'antisémitisme,* himself an agnostic Jew, seems to discern the reason for anti-Jewish hatred in beliefs and superstitions, as well as in the effect of the calamities and of the catastrophic events which afflicted the Christian peoples.

F. Lovsky, a fervent Christian, sees in the Jews only that which distinguishes them from the other peoples; a mystery which hides or reveals a divine intent. With sincerity and courage he fights against that anti-Semitism which he describes as 'a wound, secret or visible, oral or material, deliberate or blind, inflicted in the person of the Jews upon the divine will ... Whether it hide behind an economic mask, an intellectual, religious, scientific or national mask, whether it advance reasons which can at times be partly true, whether it invoke secondary causes deluding itself that they be primary ones, anti-Semitism in the end always comes back to this: it is a revolt, carried out to the detriment of the Israel of the past, the present and the future, against the plans of God as revealed in the scriptures.' But he goes on to admit this: 'Israel and Christian Hope are so profoundly linked that the more Christianity settles down, quietly and victoriously, in its temporal conquests, the more it becomes inevitable that Israel be maintained in a state of unquiet and humiliating defeat ...'

The fate of the Jews is not the result of a mystery—divine, diabolical or of any other nature—but it cannot be denied that it is exceptional, probably indeed unique, upon our planet. This unique state of affairs does not suffice to explain the hatred that has pursued and does pursue the Jews, but if we are to understand this hatred its unique nature must not be ignored.

Anything that distinguishes a man from his fellows is a sort of

[1] *Histoire de l'antisémitisme.* Vol. I: 'Du Christ aux Juifs de cour'. (Calmann-Lévy).

defiance. There are beings who hunt eagerly for defiance, or the feeling of being defied, since this will enable them to 'direct' the hatred that they carry about with them, just as young people bear within them a love of love. They observe and mark down the singularities of their equals and similars in order to turn them into *others*, when they are unable to find *others* outside their family, their city, their religion, their class and so on. *This psychological and social phenomenon which, notably in the Christian world, is most frequently expressed by and in anti-Semitism, exists everywhere.* It did not need and does not need Jews in order to be reborn with each new generation; but for thousands of years it has found in this particular ethnic and religious group an inexhaustible source of fuel for its fires.

3

Some three thousand eight hundred years ago one large family, which claimed for ancestors Abraham, Isaac and Jacob, began to be distinguished from the rest of the known world by its refusal to accept paganism, notably to accept idolatrous practices which, little changed in their true nature, are still to be encountered everywhere. *Henotheism*, that is to say the belief in a single god, was at that time fairly widespread among the nomadic Semites. But why did not Israel, while living in the land of the Pharaohs, submit to the powerful gods of Egypt, either under the Hyksos dynasty or later when, having lost their early privileges, the descendants of Joseph were reduced to the status of slaves? When, after the exodus, they set out once again upon their long migration, they chose as sacrifices to Elohim the animal gods of their former masters. The rupture became irreparable when Moses transformed henotheism into Jahvist monotheism. On the long road that led them to the conquest of the land of Canaan, and finally to the foundation of a united kingdom, they encountered, in the most varied forms, Baal and Istar, the gods of that country. The temptation to accept these gods was often almost irresistible, but each time Jahvism won the day, thus preventing them from adapting their way of life to that of the indigenous inhabitants. David's victory seemed to justify this strange religious separatism, for it was a triumph in the 'wars of Jehovah'. However, true and complete national unity was only to last for two generations; the secession took place under David's grandson. When the kingdom of the secessionists was destroyed by the Assyrians, the deported tribes submitted to the conquerors' gods and disappeared, being rapidly absorbed among the peoples of the empire. But Judah, conquered in its turn by Nebuchadnezzar and deported to Babylon, remained faithful to the Law of Moses. Then was revealed for the first time that enduring attitude which, instead of compelling universal admiration, provoked first awkward astonishment and finally hatred among 'normal' peoples; the Jews, conquered according to all the rules, bowed down and submitted to the will of their conquerors, but refused to kneel before their gods. It was discovered that they never considered themselves as being truly conquered, but believed on the contrary that a final triumph was promised to them, a triumph which would be definite. They claimed that they had one invincible ally, their God, the only true God, who reigned over all the universe—at Nineveh, at Rome, at Alexandria, as at Shiloh, Bethel or Jerusalem.

This concept of a God who was simultaneously universal and yet linked exclusively to one tiny people, this inconceivable absurdity, was a defiance of the commonsense of the polytheists. It was a superstition, an intolerable insult, or so thought men such as Tacitus and Seneca. Seneca expressed his views with a rage which has not ceased to roar through the countless perorations of the anti-Semites: 'The conquered have given laws to their conquerors.' This philosopher, a great landed proprietor and the owner of countless slaves, was, it seems, particularly irritated by their pernicious propaganda in favour of one day of rest each week. Dying in the year A.D. 65, he could not foresee that 'Jewish laziness' would one day succeed in imposing the biblical Sabbath on the Roman Empire.

The psalmist sang: 'The peoples will say: where is he then, your God?' It is a question that never ceased to be asked by all the conquerors of this little country situated in a corridor that separated all the great competing empires which surrounded it. The invisibility and anonymity of the Jewish God were all the less bearable in that they remained unimaginable. Failure to understand a secret, the existence of which appears certain, first excites distrust before inflaming hatred.

'Show us the picture, the statues of your god; we will make him whatever sacrifices he prefers', the invaders repeatedly said; and in their impatience they cut a path through to the very heart of the temple. They found nothing there; they should have then admitted that there was no secret, that they had not been lied to. But Tacitus himself—who knew the deceptive outcome of these sacrilegious incursions, and who of course could conceive of the idea of an unincarnate god taking no form perceptible to the senses—even Tacitus tended to believe that there was nevertheless some sort of a secret, and he chose the following explanation: 'The Jews,' he wrote, 'worship the gilded head of an ass.' (Others, loyal to pagan logic, were to affirm that the god of this little people was a pig; they sought to prove this by the fact that Jews are strictly forbidden to eat of its meat.) The great Roman historian who submitted to every demand that the Emperors made of him (despising them secretly but venerating them publicly as gods) raged against the contemptible aberrations of a people who obstinately refused to accept any of the superstitions that even the most broadminded intellectuals of Rome had to swallow. Thanks to the privileges accorded them by Julius Caesar, privileges which most of the pagan Emperors were to confirm in years to come, the Jews were usually granted a dispensation from taking part in the cult of the state gods, and were thus not compelled to abase themselves before the mediocre sculpture of Rome. Tacitus was all the less ready to forgive them this privilege, in that he and his fellows could not avoid such worship without risking their pleasant position in society.

Jules Isaac, who denies the existence of any 'eternal' anti-Semitism, quotes many examples of the hostility that the Jews encountered in the ancient world. This was usually inspired by the discomfort so easily provoked in connection with anything that is incomprehensible, by the religious 'separatism' of the Jews, and by their refusal to take part in that syncretism which allowed the reconciliation of all the divinities and the banishment of none; later, by the constant and repeated rebellions of the Palestinian Jews who, unlike all the other peoples, seemed definitely incapable of behaving according to the rules that vanquished peoples accept; finally, by the ubiquity of this people, for apart from the Jewry that had been reestablished in Palestine at the time of Ezra and Nehemiah, Jewish communities existed in almost every part of those territories which were later to be incorporated into the Roman empire. The idea that the Jewish dispersal began only after the year A.D. 70 is one of those pious legends which have nourished Christian anti-Semitism.[1] In fact the first anti-Jewish texts (inspired by a hatred as total as that which animated the anti-Semites of the Christian era) were the work of the inhabitants of Alexandria. Manetho and, later, Apion (this latter probably of Greek origin) wished to destroy the partially privileged position enjoyed by the Jewish communities in Egypt, and indeed elsewhere throughout the Empire; the Jews resident in Palestine doubtless worried them considerably less. (At this same period there is evidence of strong currents of contemptuous dislike being directed against the Greeks who, in their turn, had a tendency to establish themselves in communities outside their own country. They were accused of being intolerably arrogant in intellectual matters, and also of possessing too much social mobility. It is true that in order to recognise their own gods the Hellenes had only to discover their true names beneath the multitude of synonyms with which foreigners invested them. The Greeks have always insisted on their own superiority over other peoples, but have refrained from posting a similar claim on behalf of the pensionaries of Mount Olympus.)

It seems probable that Judaism would have disappeared after the terrible massacres of A.D. 70 and A.D. 135, if the Jews of the Diaspora had not preserved their religious identity. Jehovah, however, needed neither temple, nor sacrifices; he followed his faithful into exile. To affirm the Mosaic Faith a Jew needed only

[1] *Genèse de l'antisémitisme*, (Calmann-Lévy).

to live according to the Commandments, to know the Teaching (Torah) and to carry out good works. His real country, impenetrable to the strongest and best armies, was the Law. The Law and the Promise of the prophets.

Without forgetting its past, Israel, alone among peoples, drew its force from an eschatological hope, the expectation of a future near or far which, in the midst of the most appalling disasters, promised that Israel would survive. The Law, which made Israel opposed to the whole pagan world, was a heavy burden to bear, but as a protection against the seductions and perils that were all about it, Israel still had the Promise. Without prophetic messianism, Israel would inevitably have been lost. The other peoples dreamed of life in death, while Israel alone dreamed of outliving death. The others developed, to the point of mania, the cult of the dead and of death; Israel developed the cult of the future—and of the universal reconciliation of all created beings with their Creator who, at the end of time, would cause death itself to die.

Now anti-Semitism, that is to say the total hatred of the Jew, is also a result of the triumph which prophetic eschatology enjoyed over the pagan world. This world was converted to a Jehovah, who, it was said, had at last kept his promise and sent the Messiah down on earth in the form of His Own Son, whose death would redeem all those who believed in Him. The glory of Constantine finally converted the pagans, and Jehovah was installed in the temples from which the indigenous gods were now expelled. His chosen people became intolerable to the adherents of the new faith, because that people continued to await the arrival of the Last Days (Isaiah). They proudly refused to admit an incarnate god enclosed within the bounds of a mortal being. Observing this world which was supposed to have been redeemed, the Jews quoted Isaiah: 'Nation shall not lift up sword against nation, neither shall they learn war any more.' But men were still suffering and making others to suffer, killing and dying: 'No, redemption is far away, the road will be long', they said.

It was this absolute refusal to compromise the eschatological future which brought to birth the hatred manifest in 'eternal' anti-Semitism; for this was a question of vital importance: *the question of that identity which lies at the root of all true hatred.* If the refusal of the Jews was justified, then the Christians, who pretended to be the real Jews now that the Messiah had come, were either dupes or monstrously blasphemous impostors. (Pagans cannot be blasphemers, but are simply ignorant as are newborn babies.) If the Jews were wrong, then it was essential that they be compelled to recognise their folly and to renounce once and for all their pretensions of being that which they are: the bearers of the message, the people of Jehovah, the cradle of David and of the Redeemer himself.

The neophyte Gentiles, uninterested in theological matters, yet understood that their conversion implied their submission to the God of the Jews, and as a result they approached the Jewish communities wherever these existed in sufficient strength, anxious to participate in their festivals and their prayers, eating at their tables and accepting from them instruction in the faith of Jacob and of David. There had already and for many years been Judaized gentiles: these 'godfearing' people in Rome, Greece, Egypt and elsewhere believed in Jehovah without accepting the daily and difficult practice of the Mosaic Law. When Christianity triumphed and the official polytheism of the Empire was abolished, there were great openings for Jewish proselytism, which began openly to compete with the Christian Church, whose authenticity it denied and whose claims it refused to accept. It was at this point that in the name of the Religion of Love the screeches of hatred first began to be heard. They were never to be silenced again. Driven across the world, the Jews were to hear them echoing and re-echoing wherever they set foot.

Here is one such voice—emerging from a mouth that was to be called 'the mouth of gold': 'Brothel and theatre, a synagogue is also a cave full of brigands, the lair of wild beasts . . . living for their bellies, their mouths always agape, the Jews behave no better than swine or goats, living a life of lewd coarseness and excessive gluttony. They know only one way to behave: to gorge themselves and to make themselves drunk . . .' Thus spoke a priest of Antioch, a future Bishop of Constantinople, a father and saint of the Church, John Chrysostom (345-407), his intention being to expel the Jews once and for all from humanity. He was not expressing popular sentiments; quite the contrary, he was frenziedly anxious to stir up a hatred which did not yet exist. He and his like, invested with an excessive authority, were to spread this hatred throughout the Christian lands.

Nevertheless it would be unjust to see in John Chrysostom only the precursor of Julius Streicher and of Joseph Goebbels. This ascetic priest was fighting a war on two fronts, a war which he lost. He was finally exiled as a result of his attempts to combat the paganisation of the Church. He would not have expressed his hatred of the Jews in such murderously hysterical terms, had he not been aware of the Judaic essence within a Christianity now dangerously threatened by a pagan current which he himself was opposing in vain.

At the back of all the theological disputes, behind the innumerable heresies, there lurks one question of capital importance: that of the Second Coming. Without this, the Messianic pretensions of Christianity risked being reduced to that imposture which the Jews constantly maintained them to be. F. Lovsky quotes a Fourth Century text on this '... the Second Coming, without which it is not possible to believe in the First, because this latter has not accomplished all that has been prophesied for it. That is why the Jews themselves refuse to believe, because the prophesies concerning a glorious incarnation have not yet been accomplished, because they do not think that it is the Messiah who came down to earth in this fashion.' The author of *Antisémitisme et Mystère d'Israel* writes: 'It is notable that the hopes of the Church become more remote, in proportion as anti-Semitism grows within the Christian body. The Fourth Century, which marks the triumph of the theological anti-Semitic thesis, also sees the Christian City replacing the expectation of the eschatological kingdom in the thought and faith of the Christians. It may be asked whether the delay in Christ's Second Coming has not engendered precisely these anti-Semitic complaints' (page 163).

It may be asked? A useless question: the answer is in the facts, and the relationship between cause and effect is established beyond any reasonable doubt. Because humanity, though baptised, continued to live amidst the same terrors and miseries that had afflicted the generations before the Redemption, because the earth had not become the Kingdom of God, because death continued to exercise its absolute domination and disease had not disappeared, nor disorder, nor slavery, nor the misery of the poor, nor the pride of the powerful—for all these reasons, it was necessary to extinguish the eschatological hope and to replace it by imperative pretexts designed to frighten doubt. And it was said that it was the 'hardness of heart' of the Jews, who refused to believe in the first coming and in the divinity of their co-religionary Yechou of Nazareth, it was said that it was the crime of this people, deprived of their spiritual and terrestial heritage, which provided the sole obstacle that prevented the Second Coming. And it was stated that this 'deicide' race was accursed.

Then it became necessary to prove to the Christians that the Jews were indeed really accursed, for they did not seem to get on any worse than other peoples. Their fields and their gardens fed them when they tilled the soil; everywhere they practised their traditional crafts; they were in keen demand as mercenary soldiers and administrators; they proved themselves to be as skilled in trade and commerce as were the gentiles. So in what were they accursed? If the effects of the curse were not yet visible, then they must be made so forthwith: the Jews must be cut off in shame from the others, burdened with exceptional laws, humiliated forever, to make them appear more horrifying than lepers, more hateful than the cruellest and most cowardly criminals. Now was the time. Immense forces were to be employed with extreme energy for this purpose, a purpose however in which they were never to be entirely successful. This blinding propaganda of hatred, the effects of which are still sensible today—even where God has been dethroned—was at first linked indirectly with that extraordinary undertaking the purpose of which was to inspire a permanent terror in the souls of the faithful; the perpetual threat of hell which was to hang over and piously terrorise the Christians. This terror did not reform Christian morals, but resulted in an ever further submission of the Christians to the rule of the Church, which grew great in direct proportion to the anguish that it scattered throughout the world. The Devil, the Church proclaimed, is everywhere, and is all the more formidable when acting through his most loyal servants, the heretics and the Jews.

Nothing is calculated to display better the qualities and weaknesses of a man than the way in which he recognises or fails to recognise his failures and their true causes, the manner in which he puts these to rights or accepts them. The misery and grandeur of humanity are easily discerned in the fact that its greatest advances are usually but the indirect results of rebuffs and failures recognised and painfully made right, whereas failures which have not been recognised, and which therefore endure, continue to be proclaimed as unparalleled triumphs.

The very splendour of the cathedrals, those royal tombs of the extinct Hope, those fortresses of *ecclesia triumphans*, announced that the defeat of eschatological Christianity was now complete. Ecclesiastical Christianity no longer based its claims upon the future, upon a Second Coming, but sought its justification in the past: in the suffering of the saints who everywhere replaced the ancient local divinities. The cult of the Virgin and of the Divine Child satisfied dream requirements and nostalgia, the old goddesses of fertility and of love. Illiteracy protected the common people against those doubts that might have been raised in their minds had they been able to read the Bible. Those who protested, basing their protests upon the scriptures, were condemned as heretics and liquidated.

Nevertheless the Jews continued to exist. Possessing memories that only death could wipe out, drawing sustenance from roots deep in the Bible, they lived their lives beneath the very shadow of the cathedrals. Why were they not killed, exterminated once and for all? One of the most important answers to this question, and often the only one that applied, is as follows: since they had been deprived of the right to live, they were compelled constantly to pay for their existence, and to pay a very high price indeed. They became as a result an inexhaustible source of income for the powerful. Only a fool kills the goose that lays the golden eggs . . .

It happened now and then that only a few years after the Jews had been pillaged and chased out of one country, their return would be demanded of that other country where they had been compelled to seek refuge. In their relationship with the Jews, the Christian princes for more than a thousand years showed themselves to be unnaturally greedy for gold; they resembled in the most striking fashion that anti-Semitic caricature which is supposed to portray the Jewish prototype.

The anti-Jewish laws which had uprooted that 'hard-hearted' people economically, while forbidding it to carry out any normal trade, often left the Jews with only one possible means of earning a livelihood: lending with usury, which the Church forbade to the faithful. It is known that even in the Middle Ages the Jews were not the only usurers, but they were those who could be most easily expropriated by the powerful, who had simply to drive them from their territories. When doing this it was customary then, as indeed it still is, to make use of the *lumpen-proletariat,* those persons who are always ready to hand when sublime causes require the humiliation of certain individuals, the head-shaving of girls or the pillaging of shops and homes. When the cause to be served is unusually exalted, these looters become assassins too, serving indifferently whomsoever appeals to their rage. Their hatred, ferocious in action, is but functional, as ephemeral as the apparently passionate interest that newspaper readers devote to the sentimental troubles of a princess or a movie star.

The total hatred that anti-Semitism exploits is a more serious and more durable phenomenon. Christian theology, the policy of princes, and later the mystique of the political parties often provide it with a 'blanket ideology' which makes it appear honourable, though without giving it any reason to exist. The hatred of white Christians for black Christians can obviously not be explained in terms of religious intolerance. The author of anonymous letters, written to torment a family or the society of some small country town, does not write his letters for moral reasons, though he will usually invoke morality as a pretext that will permit him not to despise himself. Voltaire, to justify his own anti-Semitism, insisted on the alleged Judaic origin of certain characteristics of the Church; there is no evidence that he was himself aware of his own resemblance, at least in certain money matters, with the traditional Jew of caricature, notably in his behaviour with regard to that Prussian Jew whom Frederick the Great's friend believed, erroneously enough, to be incapable of self-defence. More than half the anti-Semitic pamphlets show that their authors were obsessed with money. And almost all these pamphlets reveal what the anti-Jewish publicists have called 'the Talmudic spirit', a phrase which they use to describe the treating of facts contemptuously and the deliberate perversion of the conclusions that should be drawn from these facts. No documents described and foresaw more exactly the technique of the Hitler régime than the famous *Protocols of the Elders of Zion,* a forgery based on the *Dialogue in Hell between Machiavelli and Montesquieu* written by the anti-Bonapartist Maurice Jolly.[1] This 'secret document' was intended to prove that the Jews were conspiring to dominate the world. Hitler constantly complained that he was the victim of infamous methods, methods which he developed and used himself just as soon as he had obtained power. Hatred conceals the anguish that torments it, but it does not always succeed in hiding the voluptuous pain in which it revels.

4

But whence does this anguish derive? In theological anti-Judaism it reflects the immense peril, at least potential if not realised, which threatened the identity and thus the legitimacy of a Church that wished to be catholic, universal and unique. Now a similar anguish can be detected in every individual who is obsessed by hatred: it drives the hate-filled man to find in others the guilt for that lack of self-assurance which casts long, dark and frightening shadows all about his own existence. Hence what he hates in the *other* are:

[1] Calmann-Lévy.

1. Those good qualities and characteristics which he realises, intolerably enough, that he himself lacks in part or, worse, totally. He then denigrates their value and makes them mysteriously suspect.

2. Those faults and weaknesses which he recognises in himself and of which he would like to be free. He forgives himself for them, and hides them from himself all the more easily by imagining that they are grotesquely exaggerated in the being whom he hates.

3. The superiority of the *other* in those fields where he knows himself to be desperately inferior.

4. The courage and the ability to obtain those satisfactions of which the hate-filled man dreams, but to which he dare not aspire, or which he fails to achieve.

5. The absence or the weakness or, on the other hand, the strength of the defence that the *other* shows when attacked by his persecutors. In all three cases hatred finds its reasons amply confirmed. Suspecting now a base hypocrisy concealing a contemptible cowardice, now an inexpungeable hatred.

6. Everything that could make the hated being appear sympathetic or honourable or admirable, everything that could in fact disarm hatred, is denounced as pretence, dissimulation, low cunning or consummate skill; the hate-filled man sees in this yet another proof that his victim 'objectively' deserves to be generally loathed.

7. Finally hatred, seeing its own intentions mirrored everywhere, must detect in its victims only beings themselves composed solely of envy and of murderous hatred. It is subject to *hysteron proteron;* and the words used by Mussolini when he was attacking a prostrate France, 'anticipated legitimate self-defence', are the words that suit hatred best.

In order to maintain his antilogical system unshaken, the hate-filled man excludes hermetically all arguments not designed to strengthen his position. It is not that he repress contradictory evidence: he is incapable of perceiving it. In order to disfigure reality, he reasons in the manner of certain psychotics, a form of

reasoning that is common incidentally to all totalitarian propagandists:

'It appears that every German pretends to know at least one
good Jew. What madness! Were this true, it would mean that
there were as many Jews in Germany as there are Germans. But
there are only half a million, and that is half a million too many!'
(The Nazi press in 1933.)

'It has been proved that the German doctors working for the
Nazi régime committed crimes against their political enemies. A
man must therefore be a Fascist if he refuses to admit that the
Jewish doctors in the Kremlin committed or planned to commit
identical crimes against the well-loved leaders of Soviet Russia.'
(Communist propaganda before the death of Stalin.)

'If it were true that Hitler had killed all those Jews, they
wouldn't be here to make these charges. Their charges are the
very best proof that they are lying.' (Whispered propaganda
since 1945.)

It is certain that bad-faith plays its part in this sort of argu-
mentation, as in all the other slanderous and libellous frenzies
that emanate from totalitarian hatred, but we would misun-
derstand the very meaning of this phenomenon if we were to
ignore the paranoiac logic which lies behind it. It reverses the
relationship between cause and effect, it dissociates facts and
pieces them together again arbitrarily. It ignores, denies or
destroys all evidence opposed to its preconceived interpretation
of events; it endows the man who applies this 'logic' with
unalterable good faith and the certainty of having seen through
the best-hidden secrets of his enemies. Let us imagine someone
objecting to Goebbels' statement in these terms: 'One person can
easily know ten, twenty, a hundred or more men; it is thus
perfectly possible that every German citizen knows and admires
at least one Jew.' To this a Nazi would reply: 'You are advancing
all these figures solely in order to confuse me. Why don't you
admit that you have been bought with Jewish gold?' And if a man
were to object: 'The example of the Nazi doctors serving their
government proves absolutely nothing in the case of the Jewish
doctors whom you accuse, on the contrary, of having acted in

contradiction to their professed opinions and in opposition to a régime which they have always served with total and obsequious devotion.' A Stalinist replies to this: 'By expressing these doubts about the perfect regularity of Soviet justice you are proving that you are a Fascist. And the fact that you, a Fascist, choose to defend those 'white coated assassins' would suffice to prove, if further proof were needed, that they are guilty.'

The logic of hatred has two main procedures, totalisation and atomisation. The anti-Semite hunts through his daily paper looking for the names of Jewish crooks, and such crooks are the only ones whose names he notices. He begins by saying that all crooks are Jews, and he totalises his generalisation into: 'All Jews are crooks.' Then he atomises; the Jews cease to be real people and are reduced to being merely the criminal acts of which he accuses them. This is the same procedure which allows totalitarian régimes to disintegrate their real and potential adversaries to the point that those adversaries become nothing save a criminal opinion, which is then 'objectively' materialised by the retro-active creation of an adequate criminal past. The man of hate effectively depersonalises the person whom he hates; by means of 'brain washing' the totalitarian régime succeeds in carrying out this atomisation in its 'practice', a process highly praised by those idealistic philosophers who, belatedly, have discovered that totalitarian infamy is the Revolution, the real Revolution.

That one man cannot permanently hate another without first dehumanising him is a cardinal fact which suggests that total hatred is a malady, or at least a partial dementia. The hateful man hates those whom he has disfigured; he has disfigured them in order that he may hate them. But why? In order to find in the absolute denial of their value the absolute confirmation of his own. Here is the 'mysterious' link which makes of anti-Semitic Christianity simultaneously the persecutor and the prisoner of Judaism; which makes Hitler say: 'There can only be one chosen people. If the Jews are that, then what are we, we Germans?'; which makes the 'white trash', the Caucasian plebeians of the southern United States, the guardians of white supremacy. (The two men who, undoubtedly in order to prove their own virility, assassinated a coloured boy because he had insistently stared at the wife of one of them, proved the existence of a characteristically 'white' fear that they were somehow and for some reason sexually inferior to the 'race of slaves'. They pretended that they were saving a woman's honour, but in fact it was out of vengeance for this incurable sentiment of sexual inferiority that they committed their murder.)

The hate-filled man is far less interested in destroying than in being in a position to despise the person whom he wishes to devalue. His greatest triumph would be achieved on that day when the hated being finally surrendered and openly despised himself. In this case his hatred would become somewhat soothed, and would even perhaps be allowed to rest.

Now anti-Semitism has never known a victory of this sort. At certain periods it has succeeded in compelling the Jews to adopt a humble attitude which it has subsequently presented as one of their 'eternal' characteristics, imposing upon them an abject attitude intended to make them appear both base and ridiculous. Even then, however, anti-Semitism could never doubt that it had failed: for the humiliated Jews preserved the pride of their faith, for which they were prepared to die. 'Since they do not despise themselves, they undoubtedly are concealing an infinite contempt for us,' thus spoke the anti-Semites. In this matter, and in this matter alone, they were not mistaken, at least when dealing with Jews who accepted as a conscious choice the destiny to which the chance of birth had exposed them.

It was not until the nineteenth century, when the tendency towards assimilation began to be strongly felt among those who now preferred to call themselves 'Israelites' rather than Jews, that the despisers succeeded at last in finding accomplices in the very ranks of their victims. In order to justify the breaking of the ties that had attached them to their fellows, certain 'assimilating' Jews sometimes went so far as to find arguments for their behaviour in the writings of their persecutors. The sort of Jew appears who seems to regard himself with the eyes of the anti-Semite; searching for his own alienation, he ends up by hating everything in himself which reminds him of his origins. It is in the person of this deserter that the anti-Semite finds at last the witness he has long been looking for, a false witness.

Every persecuted minority can invariably convince itself that its enemies know almost nothing about its true nature. This truly astonishing ignorance which has always characterised the anti-Semite is one of the most substantial reasons for the contempt that the Jews feel for their enemies. Another derives from the constatation, only too often verified, that the anti-Semite, more than any other man, deserves the reproaches that he levels at those whom he hates. What is to be thought of the charge of ritual murder, aimed so often at the adherents of a religion that categorically forbids all consumption of blood, no matter what its origin nor in what form? 'According to their dogma, it is the Christians who drink the blood and eat the flesh of their Redeemer. Must there not be some link between this profoundly pagan rite and the absurd slander that they cast at us? And each time that the body of a murdered child was found, its murderers were discovered to be among our most ferocious persecutors.' Thus thought the Jews. Even when they trembled before their enemies, they never forgot that these were often far more suitable objects for contempt than for hatred. They suspected early on that anti-Semitism was a form of contempt which constantly failed, and which sought its compensation for this in the violence that goes with total hatred.

A Jewish boy or girl is pursued through the streets of a provincial town in Poland or Moravia or Austria by a crowd of gentiles, children or even adults, spitting at him and shouting, in Yiddish, words which are in fact the affectionate diminutive for father or mother: '*Tatteli! Mammeli!*' What can such a child think of its pursuers, save contempt for them and for their savage ignorance? And this emotion will protect the child from that hatred which otherwise must have been created within him.

Is there anything more pitiful and debased than the sort of humour in which hatred seeks its relaxation? That of the anti-Semite, for example, is chiefly concerned with laughing at biblical first names, and is triumphant when it can insinuate that

John is really called Isaac—as if John, Matthew, Joseph, Michael, Mary, Ann and so on were Germanic or Celtic names ... An anti-Semite believes that he has scored a great polemical point when he is in a position to prove that the philosopher Bergson should really have been called Berekson after his ancestor Berek, a Polish Jew; or when he can reveal that the uncle of a minister was a *khazan*, that is to say the cantor in a synagogue. In order to give rise to delirious hilarity in S.S. circles, all that was necessary was a simple repetition of the name Rebecca ...

Since 1945, no man has the right to pretend he does not know that anti-Semitism is a total hatred, tending toward genocide and practising this as soon as circumstances are favourable. Anti-Semitism can be the 'socialism of imbeciles' or the fervent expression of a Christianity suffering from a bad conscience; it can be the snobbery of a disappointed, mediocre nobility, or the resentment of ill-favoured men in our industrial society; it can be the consolation of those who, being aware of how little they are, seek comfort in the existence of that which they are not (they are not Jews); it can be a weapon in the hands of those anxious to seize power or to hold on to it; it can be the last promise offered to looters, murderers and ambitious failures; it can be a radical, religious or chauvinistic *allophobia*, claiming to be either revolutionary or counter-revolutionary—it may be any or even all of these, but it is also a total hatred which becomes collective whenever social or political forces appeal to it. For hatred will become attached to whatever object is placed in its path. Thus in these last few years has been brought to birth a sort of anti-Americanism which, in many respects, is close to anti-Semitism. In both cases it is a question of an attempt to conceal the true causes of real calamities. And in both cases it is also a question of concealing the true responsibility, of providing suffering men with a guilty object, of offering them a scapegoat.

Anti-Semitism has not been disarmed. Compromised by its crimes and by those filthy practices of which it boasted for so long, it seemed to wish to disappear after Hitler's death. But hatred is reborn with each new imposture invented to exploit the misery of men's souls and bodies. The impostors borrow from hatred the appearance of their strength—from that hatred which itself is a contemptible misery, a cowardice too cowardly to admit its own existence.

Attempts can be made to cure total hatred when it is an individual phenomenon by means of therapeutic re-education. But to struggle against it when it is a social phenomenon means to combat all the impostures, religious, social and national, which an age conjures up whenever it hesitates to look its real problems straight in the face.

POSTSCRIPT

Extract from a letter to a Christian colleague:

'. . . yes, the philo-Semitism inherent in what you wrote worries me, and humiliates me as would a compliment based upon an absurd misunderstanding—a compliment that one would rather not have deserved.

'You dangerously overestimate us Jews, and you insist on loving our entire people. I do not ask, I decidedly do not wish, that we be loved in this fashion (we, or for that matter any other people). All I ask of you is justice, nothing else, nothing more. In the name of that justice I proclaim our right to number among us professional and emotional criminals, brutes of every description, ignoble men and women. A man who would refuse us this inalienable right, given to all the other peoples, condemns us to a shameful death.

'The pitiless battle against anti-Semitism is your concern. For if this hatred is sometimes a mortal danger to us, for you it is a disease, a cancer, that you carry about within yourselves. It has made us suffer horribly but we continue to overcome it, each day. The proof of this? We are free of all hatred towards you, and we feel ourselves fraternally linked with you in the defence of all those values which justify the presence of man here on earth.

'Anti-Semitism may flay our bodies, but every day it gives the lie to all your Christian aspirations. It proves their continual and daily failure.

' *"The world is yours, and your world is filled with murder—why? God is just: He makes us the victims, but He makes you the executioners."*

'You reproach me for these words which I put into the mouth of a young Jewish boy, dying at the hands of his Christian brothers-in-arms. You recall the terrible deeds of which my ancestors were guilty long ago in the land of Canaan. This is unnecessary, for I have not forgotten. That is why I do not imagine for one instant that my people is any less capable than the others of practising total hatred. But we have never pretended to be "new men", quite the contrary, for we have never ceased to affirm that the Messiah has not yet come . . .'

February 1956

THE MISERIES OF PSYCHOLOGY
to Constantine FitzGibbon

1. The Psychologist and his Past

Psychopathology came long before psychology; it is constantly practised in primitive societies, where suffering is believed to be the result of a conflict with a spirit defied by the sufferer, often without his knowing this and always without his wishing to do so. Such societies believe in the existence of the dead, of spirits who are everywhere at all times and who are gifted with a sovereign power. In curing the sufferer, magic restores him to himself; it delivers him from a state in which he was quite simply *possessed* by a spirit. Being possessed, the person had ceased to be himself, a body belonging in the present, and had become a part of that *other*. The first and most important step, therefore, was to discover who this *other* was, to reconcile him with his prey or, by means of exorcism, to force him to abandon it. In animist medicine every illness is an alienation, a conquest made by the past—and this becomes final when the issue is death.

This psychopathology is used to uncover the secret carried within him by the sick man who does not know what it is (in this too he resembles the tragic hero) or does not understand it. If he cannot recover this essential part of himself, secretly stolen or alienated from him, he will die; for it is through this alienated part that the past, the power of the dead, enters him in order to expel him from the present in which he has been living hitherto.

All suffering attacks man in his one axiomatic certainty: that of being an unshakeable unit, an indivisible whole. When he suffers he discovers that there is something *within* him which nevertheless is not *of* him. Astonished by what he does and by what he suffers, he finds himself projected into a course of action which threatens to break his unity. Now the very first step taken by the man who would regain an alienated portion of his being has this result: it shakes his certainty in his own structural wholeness and in his temporal continuity. He knew himself to be a continent, but he now discovers he is merely an archipelago; he thought he was the master of time, and he discovers instead that time can cut him into fragments.

'Know thyself!' This precept, though grammatically simple, is psychologically complicated. Is the person to whom this instruction is addressed identical or not with the person whom he is told to know? What is the relationship between the one and the other? What will he be after knowledge has been achieved? Is it a question of learning that of which we have hitherto been ignorant, or of understanding that which we already know but without comprehension? Is it the knowledge of knowledge that we must look for, the consciousness of ourselves that we must aim at, or the consciousness of consciousness? But how can we admit the existence of a consciousness unconscious of itself, of a knowledge that does not know of its own existence?

The answer given by the psychopathology of primitive men is as follows: the man possessed does not know what possesses him, for he is the victim of a struggle and of a secret vengeance. The therapeutic of the psycho-analysts seeks, as does magic, to perform a cure by abolishing the past, which it believes can be achieved by a re-presentation of what the sufferer has lived through. The sick man, reliving his past in laboratory conditions, assimilates that past instead of refusing to accept it. His consciousness becomes total and true; hitherto it was only partial, in both senses of that word. On the other hand psychiatry was scarcely interested at all in the content of the anguishes afflicting the sufferer, in his deliria or in his hallucinations, because their lack of sense was self-evident. Believing that nonsense is the constant characteristic of mental malady in all its forms, it did not look for a meaning, the existence of which it denied *a priori*.

LAY MYSTICISM

Now nonsense is only tolerable in religious communities, where it forms part of the secret that veils the inscrutable ways of the divinity. But when religions are transformed into disciplines of dogma that dessicate souls instead of exalting them, real mysticism appears upon the scene—a mysticism that aims at removing the veil from every mystery, at substituting for nonsense the meaning that lies hidden behind it, and at imposing upon God an intimacy with man obfuscated by no more secrets.

A debased mysticism, made available to all, is the almost invariable reply by which society (or the Church) would be rid of that true mysticism which, at least in the beginning, is the revolt of a faith that has lost patience waiting for those revelations promised for the end of time.

The nineteenth century produced that curious phenomenon which is foreshadowed only in one other period, that of Socrates; a mysticism without God, a philosophy which would set itself up as the science of a conquering consciousness, Hegelianism, Marxism and the different systems dealing with the psychology of the unconscious. However, whereas the natural sciences look for truth in detail without ever pretending to seize truth as a whole, lay mysticism begins the other way about. Not content with having solved this or that secret, it alleges that it possesses the key which will permit the unlocking of every secret. The knowledge elaborated by the other sciences is, for it, only fragmentary—it wishes to impose that consciousness which subsumes and resumes all forms of knowledge.

Religious mysticism always ends face to face with the agonizing question that should have been asked before it set out upon its long journey; who is it who conceals the real meanings, who has an interest in so doing? And the answer comes: it is the Devil. Or if it is God, then the Devil is God. Thus almost all mysticism is finally revealed as Satanic. It becomes in part the pathology of a twilight divinity, omnipotent and yet the prisoner of evil, the source of a poisoned love; and in part a therapeutic which attempts by unusual acts to re-establish absolute purity and to redeem the creature by redeeming his creator.

Lay mysticism can apparently dispense easily enough with God, but not with the Devil. Marxist demonology, easily transformed into totalitarian mysticism, is well known. And according to Freud, too, the Devil is there, pushing the human being towards a diabolical paradise from which he can only escape by an act of violence which will atrociously damage his consciousness.

THE CAPTIVE GUARDIAN

For orthodox Marxists and Freudians alike, history begins with Paradise Lost. According to historical materialism the human conscience, having long been distorted and disfigured due to the action of the ruling classes, evolves and grows according to the development of the means of production, becoming at last free, complete, and 'true', with the abolition of all social class. This is finally achieved by the establishment of a new paradise, on a level incomparably higher than that of the original Communist society (*Urkommunismus*). According to psycho-analysis, each generation encounters the Devil afresh in the Oedipus complex, the only psychic phenomenon which it considers to be phylogenetic and ontogenetic. Paradise can never be regained by humanity moving along the roads of civilisation. Nevertheless if the subconscious could be conquered by psycho-analytical consciousness, man could live in a state of fairly comfortable compromise with his instincts, halfway between the two antagonistic principles of pleasure and of reality. (Here is a conclusion which is certainly not likely to take anybody by surprise. Wisdom is frequently startling by its choice of arguments, but seldom, save in anecdotes, by its conclusions. The sages know how to justify this: 'If you will only cease from constantly committing the same errors, we shall no longer have to repeat the same precepts over and over again. Only imbeciles regard the repetition of error as less tedious than that of unrecognised truths.')

Just as art will not reveal itself in all its depth save to those who have submitted to its yoke, so a conquering consciousness is denied to the man whom it has not definitely mastered. To that limited logic which seeks reassurance in the equation: 'the ununderstood equals the incomprehensible equals nonsense', dialectical logic, whether Marxist or psychological, replies in words that have been used by every religion: the sense is now revealed. The man who has really understood can only agree; the man who does not agree has not really understood, and is resisting the truth owing to the pressure of his unconscious, or of inadmissible interests. According to formal logic, error is the result of a perception either incomplete or falsified by an accident, or of the imperfect application of the rules that govern a healthy judgment. According to psycho-logic, error is the refusal of truth, a repression, an obstinate and interested denial.

In the physical world divergences of opinion reflect differences of experience and of knowledge; in interpretative psychology these express the opposition between two consciousnesses. In the first case it is the laws of nature which are the subject of dispute, in the second the psychologists themselves, together with their past and their passions. The psychologist is implicit in every explanation that he gives concerning man. His position in relation to the object of his research resembles only too often that of a guardian held captive by his prisoner. It is the confusion and the hopelessly entangled promiscuity in the relations between object and subject which give to this psychology its imprecise character and make of it now a therapeutic, now an art or a discipline with esoteric practices, now a sectarian school, now a philosophy of life or even a mysticism. Such relations are doubtless dialectic: it is known that the Freudian psycho-analyst must himself submit to treatment before he can achieve the right to practice. In principle only one solitary exception to this rule is admitted, one sole case where a man succeeded in understanding and in practising psycho-analysis without himself having previously been treated by another: Sigmund Freud.

'In the summer of 1897 the spell began to break, and Freud undertook his most heroic feat—a psycho-analysis of his own unconscious. It is hard for us nowadays to imagine how momentous this achievement was, that difficulty being the fate of most pioneering exploits ...

The end of all that labour and suffering was the last and final phase in the evolution of Freud's personality. There emerged the serene and benign Freud henceforth free to pursue his work in imperturbable composure.'

Thus speaks Ernest Jones, Freud's disciple, collaborator and close friend for forty years, in a work which will doubtless be considered for a long time as the definitive biography of the founder of psycho-analysis.[1]

CONQUERING CONSCIOUSNESS

As Malraux has shown, the greatness of a work of art is partly nourished by the unhappiness of him who made it, though only too often that unhappiness is not consumed in the process. The splendour of art is easily compatible with the sufferings of the artist; however, the servitude of the psychologist seems less in keeping with the liberating purpose of his psychology. If the faith does not save those who preach it, who will it save? But perhaps the apostle does not search for his own salvation, nor the psychologist for his own equilibrium. Certainly Nietzsche was looking for a regimen of the soul, but, taken all in all, this was for him little more than a secondary product of that *Umwertung der Werte,* of that overturning of the hierarchy of values, which was really the sole centre of his preoccupations. The sad cries, half pyschotic, of this Dionysos crucified, betray his longing for the salvation of the universe. He set himself up as moralist and psychologist in order to eliminate once and for all that 'metaphysical need' of which he thought to have freed himself, and to which he was to succumb in his delirium. His madness was perhaps a refuge, but it was neither salvation nor equilibrium.

'For I am not really a man of science, not an observer, not an experimenter and not a thinker. I am nothing but by temperament a Conquistador—an adventurer, if you want to translate the word—with the curiosity, the boldness and the tenacity that belongs to that type of being.'

Thus wrote Freud, not without a touch of vanity, to his friend,

[1] See *Sigmund Freud, Life and Work,* (Vol. I: *The Young Freud, 1856-1900,* pp. 351 and 352), by Ernest Jones (Hogarth Press, London, 1953). Quotations from this work will be referred to by the letters FLW, and those taken from *Aus den Anfängen der Psychoanalyse, Briefe an Wilhelm Fliess etc. von Sigmund Freud* (Imago, London, '952), by the letters FFL.

Fliess (FLW, page 382).[1] Nietzsche, too, would have felt flattered to have the word *conquistador* used about himself, as would Stendhal, and the predecessor of them all, la Rochefoucauld. The *terra incognita,* conquered in the very moment of its discovery, is man, that most secretive of animals and the most skilled in the defence of that which he hides even from himself. He must be stripped naked—*entlarven* was Nietzsche's word—unmasked. It is understandable that the author of *Menschliches, Allzumensch-liches* ended by announcing that the will to power is the most imperious of the virtues, indispensable if the superman is to be realised.

The conquering consciousness thus becomes the end of those who would dominate the conscious, and perhaps, thereby, everything else.

If the will to power explains much, it has even more need of being itself explained, as indeed has every exaggerated desire. And this desire demands no less than the disruption of human solidarity. The man who fears that he may become nothing save an object to all his fellows, feels a need to see them all degraded until they become mere objects for him. This is the only price by which he thinks that he can become that which he is: himself. (From the moment that Raskolnikov can only conceive of himself in the terms of a negative infinite—a louse—or a positive one—a god—he is embarked upon murder. The murderous act of Lafcadio is not gratuitous: Gide's hero kills—or wounds himself, or throws himself into a burning building—in order to prove that he alone is master of himself. Whatever the author, a naïve Nietzschean when writing *Les Caves du Vatican,* may have thought, the exploits of his young man are attempts to escape from a misery of impotence and from the fear that he may drown in nothingness. In reality Lafcadio would commit none of the actions ascribed to him, but would dream about them as a timid onanist dreams of himself in the rôle of a hero performing spectacular seductions.)

[1] It is to be noted that the letter from which Jones quotes this extract is not given in FFL, the only existent, published collection of the letters written by Freud to his closest friend.

It is thus seen that behind the will to power lies the humiliation of being human and of not being what one would desire to appear. Humiliation, more than any other form of suffering and more than any passion, drives a man to extremes. It suffices for destruction; it must be overcome if creative energy is to emerge, an energy that will dissolve the will to power and disavow it as a lost illusion. Only then will the great end be revealed: understanding. The first stage of this is that *Selbsterweiterung* of which Nietzsche spoke, that enlargement of oneself by means of which a man seems to integrate the universe into his being by understanding it. For if knowledge reveals things, understanding gives its possessor a hold over them. There is thus yet another suspect side to any passionate will to understand, a will such as is notably in evidence with every true psychologist as with every man who is not satisfied by an explanation unless it be preceded or followed by an interpretation, by the revelation of a hidden meaning.

'FICTION'

The adage, *si duo idem faciunt, non est idem,* and its inversion, 'two different acts can be identical', constitute the point of departure for all depth psychology, containing as they do the certainty that there are two forms of psychic being: the being as he is in reality and as he is in appearance. The latter is a function of the former and forms part of reality to the same extent that a lie is the characteristic expression of the person who tells it and is, indeed, in general more revealing than a true statement. The pose, the mask, the borrowed gesture, transitory though they be, reveal that which a man would wish to appear to be and, by antithesis, that which he does not desire to be: that is to say, that which he really is. Each of us crams into his being a fiction without which the image that he forms of himself would be broken, fragmentary, in fact unbearable, for it would run contrary to his vital need to know himself as a structural unity and as a justified existence.

Fear of being duped, and a steady distrust of this overlapping where the appearance and the real being intermingle, are emotions that inspire misanthropy and satire; it is not they, however, that give the psychologists their burning desire to understand, for the psychologist, like the mystic, believes that every secret can be unravelled since it carries within itself its own solution. We detect here the need to understand in order to establish one's own true position, in order to free oneself from a fiction which can amount to a slavery if it be not destroyed.

Now the appearance reflects the real being as the shadow 'reflects' the body; the body 'casts' a shadow, but only in relation to the light that it intercepts. Man can only express himself and be understood by others in his relationships; apart from them he is a dumb essence, incapable of transmission. The psychologists move from the shadow towards the body and the light, in order to discover those relationships in which the person takes on a concrete existence, and among those notably his relationship with himself, the terminology, the shorthand, the symbols which he employs in those solitary dialogues by which the 'I' affirms its identity and its continuity. (In schizophrenes, voices make this dialogue impossible, destroying identity and thus tearing apart personality.)

Every true psychology aims at the unveiling and elimination of man's fiction. When Montaigne undertook to paint his own portrait, he suspected that 'we are nothing but ceremony', and went on to play a complicated game of shadows. They alone, multiplying with distance, show the positions and the movements of a being who attempts to give himself by means of references, reflexes and reflections, but will not let himself be taken. The French moralists, the first modern psychologists, tried to establish each characteristic attitude through the shadows that both display and distort it. Rousseau placed Montaigne and indeed all his own predecessors, 'at the head of those false sincere men who would deceive by telling the truth'; Rousseau, who is without doubt the most false and the most sincere of all, was aware of the double game that he was playing. 'In surrendering simultaneously to the memory of the impression received and to present feelings about that impression, I shall paint my state of soul twice over, at the moment of the event and at the moment when I describe it.' And memory, servile as the legal system in a totalitarian state that passes retroactive laws, allows this extraordinary reconstruction based upon innumerable *as ifs,* upon a fiction according to which reality becomes a function dependent upon appearance, and the past is retroactively transformable at every moment. It happens in psychology that a man will rape the truth because he loves it, and is not sufficiently loved by it in return.

Since Rousseau we have known that the true answer to the question: 'Who am I?' is not to paint a portrait of one's being but to write a history of one's becoming. Hegel, more strongly influenced in his youth by Rousseau than by any other modern thinker, understood this best of all. His philosophy of becoming was to inspire the sociology of becoming, as formulated by Marx. Similarly a thread links the author of the *Confessions,* by way of Dostoievsky, Charcot and Nietzsche, with the founders of interpretative psychology; and there is a profound relationship between the misery of Jean-Jacques and the misery which is sometimes put to rights by the art of the psychologist, although his science is intended solely to define it.

---

2. Freud and his Psyscho-analysis

The Origins

He was born on the 6th of May, 1856. Thus the founding father of psycho-analysis was a member of the only peaceful generation that Europe has produced for the last two hundred years; that of the men born after 1848 and before 1870. Their youth and the best years of their maturity were passed before 1914. Too old to be seriously threatened by the Great War, they lived through it serenely enough, before confronting the new century which was born in 1918.

In the domain of the spirit, in the sciences as in the arts, no subsequent generation has shown such boldness as those peaceful men whose way of life was bourgeois enough, frequently marked by an easy conformism, but whose actions prepared or carried out a revolution in traditional habits of thought, of research and of creation. The extraordinary speed of economic expansion had as one of its results to endow the sons of rich middle class men with a pseudo-aristocratic style, while opening to the talent and energy of the children of the lower middle classes a whole universe for their discovery and conquest.

Freud was the son of a Jewish couple from Eastern Galicia, migrating steadily westward, pushed simultaneously by the desire for a decent material existence and even, if lucky, wealth, and by the hope of escaping from humiliation. Freiberg in Moravia, where Amalia Nathanson, second wife of Jacob Freud, gave birth to her eldest son, was only one stage along the road that finally took this family to Vienna. Their hopes were not to be realised. The father remained all his life 'waiting, full of confidence, for something to turn up'. Poverty, made only just tolerable by the subsidies that the mother's family sent her, haunted the childhood and youth of Sigmund. Even when he had finished his studies, he still needed financial assistance; he received this from a Jewish colleague, Doctor Joseph Breuer, his friend and guide during his formative years. 'I have been poor and defenceless, and I continue to fear this all the time,' he was to say, even at the age of forty-three (FFL, page 319).

The Hapsburg Empire had long been declining with the splendour of a summer's sunset, and was only to be extinguished after the death of an Emperor who had reigned without interruption for sixty-eight years. His capital, one of the great crossroads of Europe for more than a millenium, seemed to promise everything to everybody: emancipation to the sons of peoples less oppressed than bullied, exquisite new delights to luxury-loving provincials, and to the ambitious wealth, fame and even the achievement of power.

Freud as a young man must be counted among the ambitious. 'The childhood phantasies and the adolescent day dreams of Freud, as far as we know them, do not foretell the future originator of psycho-analysis. They fit a general, a reformer, or

a business executive rather than the patient, full-time listener
to petty complaints, humdrum stories and the recounting of
irrational sufferings. It was a long way from the child who
devoured Thiers' story of Napoleon's power, who identified
himself with the Marshal Masséna,[1] Duke of Rivoli and Prince
of Essling, to the psycho-analyst who cheerfully admits that he
has, in fact, very little control even over those symptoms and
disturbances which he has learned to understand so well.
Twelve years old, he still thinks of himself as a candidate for
cabinet rank and, as an adolescent, he plans to become a lawyer,
and to go into politics. Then, at seventeen, shortly after his
graduation from high school, Freud suddenly retreats from his
power over men ... Power, prestige, and wealth should come
to him only contingent to his being a great scientist' (S.
Bernfeld, quoted FLW, page 33).

His aspirations were in proportion to the humiliating circumstances in which he was brought up, their intensity corresponding
to a situation determined by his origin, his uprooted condition
and a fundamental disruption in his nature.

VIENNA AND THE INTRUDERS

Vienna, where Freud lived from his fourth to his eighty-second
year (when, in 1938, he was forced to become an expatriate), was
the most anti-Semitic of all the great cities in the world. Hatred
of the Jews took a thousand forms, but always preserved an
undeniable quality of opportunism: it was weak, almost non-
existent, so far as the strong were concerned and strong, even
violent, when directed against the defenceless weak. None was
ever weaker than those Jews from Eastern Europe who came to
Vienna in a desperate search for the bread with which to feed
their families, and for a fortune and great careers for their
children. Their naked poverty gave rise to contempt, their

[1] This identification with Masséna was due to a mistake: Freud believed
that the Marshal had been born on May 6th, 1756, that is to say exactly
one century before himself, and, furthermore, that he was Jewish.

ambition to fear, the success of their sons to envy, the strangeness of their customs and the obsessive fervour of their faith to an unbearable feeling of disquiet. The lower middle classes turned against them that resentment which they felt for the rich native Jews living in their fine houses; and the rich Jews themselves would have preferred to see a barrier less easily crossed than the Danube Canal between themselves and that quarter called Leopoldstadt where the immigrants from the East first settled. Freud was to live for seventy-eight years in a city which he never loved, frequently hated and always despised. 'I hate Vienna as though it were a person and, unlike the giant Antaeus, I derive new strength as soon as my foot touches a soil other than that of my native city' (FFL, page 333). 'Vienna remains Vienna, that is to say disgusting in the highest degree' (FFL, page 340).

Freud was a child of Leopoldstadt. Numerous indications of his private life are to be found scattered throughout almost all his writings. These are hints rather than admissions, for nowhere does he disclose the secret that he was of Galician origin. The famous incident of his father being humiliated by an anti-Semite, and compelled to step off the pavement into the gutter, is badly told by Freud, for he conceals the fact that this took place in Galicia where his father still wore, on the Sabbath, the *streimel*, a sort of fur hat, a really ridiculous garment, provocative of insult, that the Polish nobility had ordered the Jews to wear in years gone by. This incident, an everyday occurrence in the eyes of the father who was its victim, assumed a great importance in the eyes of the son: he was never again to recognise the authority of this man who had not known how to defend himself against humiliation.

The rootlessness of the immigrants, and the steady influence of the strange world in which the child slowly began to settle down, made possible, if not inevitable, at least relatively easy, that rupture which now took place: Freud abandoned the faith which was the foundation and the imperative content of his people's life. Such an abandonment is in many cases accompanied by the destruction of all the links attaching the younger generation to that of its fathers; it often has the effect of freeing ambition from every moral restraint, of damming all the springs where scruple rises. It is in no way comparable with that natural conflict between generations to be encountered elsewhere: it is not a matter of decades but of centuries that separate such Jews from their parents; it is the opposition of two different worlds.

For Freud this rupture did not involve an emotional break with his family. Far from trying to restrain his ambitions, his parents encouraged them, reckoning on his great future success of which they stood all the more in need since the father remained decidedly incapable of achieving anything himself. Furthermore, the child's birth had been accompanied by signs which, to the superstitious, promised a truly astonishing career: he was born with a thick head of hair; an old woman forecast that he would be a great man; a Viennese fortune teller said that he would be a minister of state.

THE PSYCHOLOGY OF THE SOUL

'Neither at that time [when he was deciding upon his future profession] nor indeed in my later life, did I feel any particular predilection for the career of a physician', Freud said. And elsewhere: 'After forty-one years of medical activity, my self-knowledge tells me that I have never really been a doctor in the proper sense ... I have no knowledge of having had in my early years any craving to help suffering humanity ... In my youth I felt an overpowering need to understand something of the riddles of the world in which we live and perhaps even to contribute something to their solution. The most hopeful means of achieving this end seemed to be to enrol myself in the medical faculty; but even then I experimented—unsuccessfully—with zoology and chemistry, till at last, under the influence of Bruecke, the greatest authority who affected me more than any other in my whole life, I settled down to physiology, though in those days it was too narrowly restricted to histology. By that time I had already passed all my medical examinations, but I took no interest in anything to do with medicine till the teacher, whom I so deeply respected, warned me that in view of my restricted material circumstances I could not possibly take up a theoretical career. Thus I passed from the histology of the nervous system to neuropathology and then, prompted by fresh influences, I began to be concerned with the neuroses' (FLW, pages 31 and 32).

These lines, which sum up the beginning of his scientific career, clearly reveal that the researches which Freud undertook were intended, at least in the mind of his masters, to end in the final elimination of psychology, which was to be absorbed into a physiology ambitious of being both a somatology and, simultaneously, an anthropology. 'There are no forces active within the organism other than those of a physical and chemical nature.' Such was the teaching of the great physiological school of which Bruecke, together with Du Bois-Reymond and Helmholtz, were the best known and most energetic representatives. This current of thought attracted young Freud through its materialistic monism, which seemed to be the most suitable philosophy with which to replace the religion he had lost, and also for the reason that physiology opened the prospect of extraordinary discoveries still to be made.

Now Freud thought that he would succeed by one brilliant stroke, that one sensational discovery would bring him position, glory and wealth. It is from his letters to Martha Bernays that we learn best to understand what were his motives and ambitions between the ages of twenty-five and thirty. (Ernest Jones, in FLW, is the first man so far to give us extracts from this correspondence.) In speaking of the influence of Bruecke, Freud gives a curiously false idea of the sources from which he derived his inspiration. Young Freud, no doubt, had good and adequate reasons for admiring his master of that period, scholar of integrity and man of courage, but the future psychologist owes nothing to him insofar as his own great work is concerned. No man did more than Joseph Breuer to show him his true road; so far as encouragement went, none was as important as Wilhelm Fliess; and as for the opening of new horizons, it was the meeting with Charcot and to a lesser extent with Bernheim that counted. His career as physiologist and neuropathologist was only an episode without any real importance so far as his future went. His

researches might have made of Freud a first class neurologist...
But nothing foreshadowed the existence of a genius, thinks his
friend Jones.

Twice the physiologist seemed upon the verge of a glorious
success, but in neither case did it amount to anything. His second
great chance came when he began to study the effects of cocaine.
He took it himself, and recommended it to all his friends, convinced that it could only have beneficial effects: a grave mistake,
which was to be the subject of reproaches levelled at him for
many years. He recognised the analgesic effects of the drug,
probably also suspected its anaesthetic action, but it was a
colleague whom he had kept informed of the course of his
researches who, utilising cocaine for ophthalmological surgery,
derived all the profit from these researches. One year later, at the
age of twenty-seven, Freud wrote to his fiancée: 'I prefer to do
without my ambition, make less noise in the world, and have less
success rather than injure my nervous system.' He was, indeed,
suffering from atrocious headaches and other nervous troubles.
'For the rest of my time in the hospital I will live like the Goys,
modestly... without striving after discoveries or reaching to the
depths' (FLW, page 178).

One of the reasons why he could never give up striving was
that in Vienna even a run-of-the-mill university career was
only possible for a Jew if he made efforts incomparably greater
than those required of the 'Goys'. Another was the influence and
friendship of Breuer; the final and decisive one—in 1885—the
journey to Paris:

'I believe I am changing a great deal, Charcot who is both one
of the greatest of physicians and a man whose common sense
is of the order of genius, simply demolishes my views and
aims... when I go away from him I have no more wish to
work at my own simple things... Whether the seed will ever
bring forth fruit I do not know; but what I certainly know is
that no other human being has ever affected me in such a way'
(FLW, page 202).

In a lecture which he delivered a few months after his return to

Vienna, he set himself up as the interpreter of Charcot's ideas. But the majority of his colleagues and notably the head of his department, the redoubtable Meynert, professor of psychiatry, refused seriously to envisage a psychogenetic etiology of hysteria. During the years that followed Freud went on with his neuro-pathological research, meanwhile translating two books by Charcot and two by Bernheim whom he visited at Nancy in order to study his technique of hypnosis.

Promoted *privat-dozent,* or approximately lecturer, he married after a long engagement made all the longer by financial worries, and finally set up a home. Electrotherapy, which he employed in the treatment of his patients, proved a disappointment; for several years he attempted cures by hypnotic suggestion, although he already knew (at least since 1882) of the cathartic method which Breuer, when handling the famous case 'Anna O.' had almost accidentally developed.

As E. Jones truly remarks, there is no sign of any intuition playing a part during this period of Freud's very slow development. Later, after his auto-analysis, he was to be carried forward, as it were by an irresistible stream, but until then he seems to have hobbled when he would have run. Already convinced of the psychogenesis of the illnesses with which he was concerned, he continued nevertheless to search for a physiology of the soul, when what he needed in fact was a psychology of the body. It was also in defence against the claims of psychology that he turned towards that sexualism which characterises his first explanations of neurotic phenomena: he was anxious to find a purely somatic (organic and functional) cause for *Angst.* Now it was precisely this sexualism which seemed to arouse the strongest resistance on the part of his former teachers and colleagues, who were determined to accept only scientific, which for them meant somatic, explanations. As for the doctors, and particularly the neurologists, they spoke with contempt of the 'theatrical spectacles' with which Charcot enlivened his courses at the Salpêtrière. Liébault and Bernheim were regarded as little better than charlatans who regaled the public with displays of hypnotism.

ISOLATION

Freud was to be a revolutionary despite himself. A liberal in politics, lacking all contact with revolutionary movements, morally strict, modest and even a prude, he was to see his name attached to that sexual emancipation which was already in the air at the end of the last century. The official, and frequently hypocritical, representatives of morality were, for decades, to attack the immoral teaching of this man who was himself a model of sexual morality. There are indeed good reasons to think that Freud remained chaste until marriage—he was thirty years old at that time—that as a husband he was a perfect example of fidelity, and that long before reaching old age he gave up every sort of sexual life. A handsome young man, and later an irresistible thaumaturge to his many female admirers and patients, he knew many temptations; he was doubtless able to overcome them. (The case of Nietzsche, that virtuous immoralist, is very different, if only because the world that he provoked was totally unaware even of his existence.)

Freud knew the loneliness that is the fate of the revolutionary despite himself. Surrounded by a steadily growing family, he became more and more lonely; tortured by his headaches, struck down by bouts of depression, his heart often threatened to give way. Weeks of furious works alternated with periods in which he felt himself drained of all strength and of all hope. His financial situation remained precarious. To increase the number of his patients, it was necessary that he be appointed professor. (When the Imperial Minister finally signed his promotion, it was thanks to the intervention of a woman of the world. But the argument that clinched the matter was the lady's promise to donate a picture to a state museum. There was one in particular that the Minister had his eye on, and its gift to the state was the best way of convincing him that the Israelite in question possessed the necessary scientific qualifications for a professorship. The picture is by Boecklin and is called *The Ruined Castle* ...)

He was now forty years old. His greying beard made him appear older than his years, but his eyes and forehead remained young beneath the thick hair of an adolescent who has matured too quickly. 'Yes, I am really forty-four years old, a rather worn out old Jew', he wrote to Fliess. 'You know how limited are my pleasures: I can only smoke inferior tobacco; alcohol means nothing to me; I have given up producing children; I have cut off all contact with my fellow men.'

Seven years earlier he had published, in collaboration with Breuer, his *Studien über die Hysterie*. Of the 800 copies printed, 180 still remained unsold thirteen years later. But now he had published *Die Traumdeutung* (The Science of Dreams), the most astonishing of his works and the one which is doubtless most redolent of genius. However 'not even the most obscure magazine published anything that could lead me to believe that *Traumdeutung* has made the slightest impression on anyone whatsoever ... I had become intoxicated with the hope that at long last I had taken a decisive step towards freedom and prosperity. The reception that the book received, this total silence, destroyed once again what might have been a new link with my environment' (FFL, pages 332-333).

This disappointed outburst is to be found in one of the last letters he was to write to Fliess. For their extraordinary friendship was already undermined. Soon all that remained was to be a bitterness softened, it is true, by the passage of time, but which the many years of a very long life were never to eradicate. A little before this break, Freud had assured his friend that nothing could ever take his place, that without the 'unique public' that Fliess was to him, his works would have neither sense nor purpose.

THE FRIEND

Friendship, common enough in childhood and youth, is more rare in the life of adults. The ability to establish new human relationships in depth is one that, with most men, decreases as they grow older. The death of friendships, whether slow or quick, leaves a scar, of which men remain generally unaware, because during this period of their life they are preoccupied with the effort of founding a family and are definitely establishing their social existence. Once these have been achieved, they reproduce their traditional relationships, or their natural ones, and begin to play the part they saw played by their parents in their childhood. In this scenario which they think they know so well, they expect only happiness, and unhappiness alone is unexpected, though its frequency is the sole plot of the play, and its absence the sole happiness of a well regulated life.

The importance that Freud attached to his friendship with Breuer is well known, but it is only now, thanks to the publication of a selection of his letters to Fliess, that we can appreciate the full depth of that other friendship, of the tragic intimacy that linked him, like a love affair of almost fifteen years duration, to the Berlin doctor. Apart from the dreams that he recounts in *Traumdeutung* and certain events in his private life which he only published in order that he might explain them, nothing published hitherto has given us such an insight as do these letters into how Freud became a psycho-analyst.

Wilhelm Fliess was an oto-rhino-laryngologist, as ambitious as his Viennese friend, a brilliant and subtle conversationalist, admired by his whole circle, who seemed destined to achieve great success in the very promising field offered by physiological research. A lay mystic inspired by the school of Helmholtz, even within the narrow limits imposed by the phenomena that he chose to study as his own speciality, he was forever searching for the key to 'the riddles of the universe'. Having discovered what he called the 'nasal neuro-reflex' and the innumerable symptoms which, in the sequel, affect other organs, notably the female genital organs and the stomach, he went on by a process of expansion and ever more audacious generalisations to reach two fundamental concepts: bisexuality is a characteristic of every organism, and periodicity controls it, from its birth to its death, governing everything that living creatures do, even their sufferings, their illnesses and their accidents. Until the day of his death Fliess remained convinced that all the secrets are to be found in the two numbers of periodicity, twenty-three and twenty-eight: his calculations came to resemble more and more the mystic algebra of the Middle Ages.

It was largely due to Fliess, whom he had met through Breuer, that Freud was inspired to search in sexuality for the origin of neuroses, a search which would enable him to explain these maladies according to a purely mechanical physiology. In the theory of bisexuality, sexualism found an indispensable and fairly satisfactory basis. Freud was also inclined to accept the hypothesis of periodicity, which his friend considered to be the keystone in the arch of his cosmic biology; but his own experiments did not seem to him to confirm Fliess's play on numbers. It may be supposed that this produced a feeling of guilt, and that he determined to try harder. But when, after their break, they were looking for respectable and admissible reasons, that is to say superficial ones, for this break, one that was to be found was the absence of periodicity from the explanations that Freud gave for hysteria.[1]

Another, and probably the decisive, reason for the row was a terrible remark that Fliess had made on the occasion of their last 'congress'[2]: he accused Freud of finding in the cases he had analysed only what he had himself put into them, and he described him as a *Gedankenleser,* a thought reader, an extremely insulting term when used by a Helmholtzian. The wound was all the more

[1] In the long dialogue that constitute the letters which these two men exchanged, we shall never be able to hear the voice of Fliess, for his letters were destroyed one and all by Freud shortly after the break. Of all that Freud wrote to his friend (letters, postcards, notes, studies) two hundred and eighty-four items have been saved, thanks to Marie Bonaparte. It is hard to agree with the editors of FFL, that they were right to leave out entirely one hundred and sixteen of these and to cut out certain passages in some of the one hundred and sixty-eight letters that they did regard it as their duty to publish. The explanation that they give of this procedure is not fully satisfactory. All the more so since it is given by psycho-analysts who are not in the habit of exercising any exaggerated discretion when dealing with men whom celebrity has turned into public figures. The suppression of passages 'which are contrary to private discretion' is arguable, but the suppression of those which deal with 'the efforts of Freud to enter into Fliess's views' seems as little justified as is the elimination of all that deals with his rupture with Breuer. Having said this, one must add that the editors of FFL, Marie Bonaparte, Anna Freud and Ernst Kris, are entitled to our gratitude.

[2] The word that Fliess and Freud used to describe their meetings.

cruel in that Fliess was doubtless referring to a phase during which Freud had gone dangerously wrong, precisely because he had been projecting his own ideas into his patients. And it was to this friend that Freud had first of all, with considerable courage and honesty,[1] admitted this failure which threatened to put an end to his entire career, and also to his 'hopes of eternal glory and of certain wealth'.

THE FICTION OF RAPE

This systematic error which led him astray for four years, that is to say until the autumn of 1897, was far more important and far more significant than the generalisations contained in his study of cocaine. It was what Nietzsche has called the typical experience (*das typische Erlebnis*), the experience which is not inflicted upon a man from outside, but which is a repeated event, unconsciously 'arranged' (Adler) whenever he comes closest to his own destiny. This experience will recur for just so long as a man refuses to recognise the warning that it carries with it.

For four years Freud led his hysterics to recount to him the capital event of their lives, and this was always the same: they had been the victims of a rape committed by their father. It was in this trauma that he found the decisive reason for hysteria. 'I believe that this is a revelation of very great importance, the discovery of the *caput Nili* of neuropathology,' he announced on the 2nd May, 1896, in a communication addressed to the Society of Psychiatry and Neurology of Vienna. And he went on to quote eighteen cases which he claimed to have analysed completely. (Old Krafft-Ebing, who presided at this meeting, summed

[1] In the third and last volume of *Sigmund Freud, Life and Work*, p. 285, Ernest Jones states that I made 'the scurrilous accusation that Freud had dishonestly concealed the fact(!) that it was he who had suggested these theories to his patients'. The reader will reach his own conclusions, but will surely see that I in no way impugn Freud's good faith: on the other hand I do maintain that his unconscious, what I have called his 'fiction', which contributed to his discoveries, was also the major cause of his mistakes.

up his own attitude in one phrase: 'A fairy tale told by a scholar.') That Freud should have looked for the cause of hysteria in one trauma is explicable partly as due to the influence of Charcot, and partly owing to the mechanistic way of thought to which he had remained faithful. And doubtless his desire to make a sensational discovery also played its part in this. Indeed the melodramatic tendencies of psycho-analysis only began to fade away during the last years of his life, when Freud was turning more and more towards psychology of the Ego, a form of psychology which, since then, has come steadily closer to Adler's theory.

In a letter of vital importance dated 21st September, 1897, and addressed to Fliess, he expressed the full bitterness of this rebuff: 'I no longer believe in my *neurotica*,' he said before going on to enumerate the facts, notably the absence of true therapeutic success, which had first caused him to doubt and finally led him to the conviction that he had been misled for far too long. He had confused the fiction produced by his patients with the real experience which he thought to rediscover in their memories. Now, neither in this letter nor in any other, neither at this time nor later, was he to insist on the one cardinal point, namely that he and he alone had first suggested to his hysterics these tales which he then accepted as definite proofs in favour of his etiology. Rape had taken place, but the fathers of his patients had had nothing to do with it: this rape formed part of a therapeutic in which the past, far more than the present, succumbed to the seductions of the analyst whose fiction it had to justify.

It is no doubt to this rape that Fliess is referring when he reproached his friend for finding nothing in his neurotics save what he himself had placed there. And it was of this too that Freud was thinking when he replied: 'You are destroying the value of my discoveries.'

Fliess, although dangerously astray so far as his own speculations went, had formulated a critique from which no system of interpretative psychology can altogether escape: the inability of the psychologist to abstract himself entirely from his own psychology creates formidable obstacles to his search for truth, a search that will be obstructed by his own fiction and by the reflection of this in the souls that he is attempting to understand.

In addition to the explanations already given for the extreme interest that Freud took in sexual phenomena there is another, of a more personal nature: the wish to overcome his own prudishness, a product of the very severe sexual morality which prevailed in the environment from which he came. Thus from the very beginning there is the question of an attempted auto-emancipation, all the more courageous in that it was to result in opposing him to his new environment. But whence comes the fiction of rape? Certainly all neurotic persons regard themselves as victims. With only the slightest encouragement, they will show that the path which leads them back towards their past is a *via dolorosa*. They will accept with pleasure the idea that they have been oppressed by those whom they loved, even from their very birth. If, as is done in literature, the innumerable petty facts ascribable to this oppression are condensed into one major fact, whether of an amorous nature or not, the result is inevitably rape, if the parable is to be expressed in sexual jargon. But what part of his being or of his fiction led Freud to suggest precisely this parable? The irresistible force of the inspiration that had led him to this endured; for even when he abandoned the theory of the rape of the child by the father, Freud maintained exactly the same position, only now he faced the opposite direction: he discovered the Oedipus Complex, that sexual desire which urges the child to possess one of its parents and to kill the other. The only real change, and that an unavoidable one, lies elsewhere: in the discernment that was henceforth his between fiction and real experience. But the number of these real experiences being practically infinite, even in the most inactive life, selection becomes necessary, even among those facts that 'free association' allows to float to the surface. Such free association is far more free than are dreams; but after a few sessions of psychotherapeutic treatment, the clients of the psycho-analysts dream psycho-analytical dreams, the clients of the Jungians dream in terms of the myth-jargon of the Collective Unconscious, while those who are being treated by Adlerians, though their dreams are far less circumscribed by clichés, will nonetheless produce ones that are agreeably acceptable to their doctors. (Neurotic resistance may wipe out the memory of dreams, but seldom prevents this curious adaptation.)

Once again Freud was looking for what he had already found, and obviously he ended by discovering it. Auto-analysis, according to his biographer, opened wide the royal road.

Now it was not in his own childhood that Freud found the Oedipus Complex. What he discovered there was this: the vitally important part that an old servant woman, as ugly as she was intelligent, had played in his life up to the age of two and a half, when she was arrested for theft and suddenly disappeared—the first rupture and one of a very great importance; he discovered too that he had been jealous of a brother born one year after himself and who had died aged only a few months; that his libido towards his mother had been awakened when, travelling with her, he had on one occasion seen her naked (describing this, Freud employs Latin words for 'mother' and 'naked'); that his father played no active rôle whatsoever in his childhood; and finally that the son of his elder half-brother, that is to say his nephew who was one year older than the uncle, had been 'the companion in his misdeeds' during his first two years, before the family had left Freiberg. 'This nephew and my young brother determined the neurotic character of all my friendships, and also their intensity' (FFL, page 223). Elsewhere Freud admits that he felt at all times the need for one intimate friend and one enemy to hate, the two being occasionally united in one and the same person.

In reading his letters it is easy enough to detect those factors from the past of which he wishes to be delivered; but what emerges even more clearly, and in the most intimate passages, is his finality, the image of the personality that he would be, the ambition that drives and tortures him.

As soon as he was sure that the woman who would be his wife loved him, he confronted her with ultimatums whenever he felt that his power over her was threatened. She had to break with her friends, with one of her brothers. And when she thought of returning to Vienna and thereby saving her mother considerable expense, her fiancé reproached her furiously for having been able to think of her mother when she should have been thinking only of him. He wrote: 'If this is so, then you are my enemy . . . If you do not succeed in overcoming this obstacle, everything between us will be wrecked. If you are not sufficiently attached to me in order to renounce your family, then you must lose me, destroy my life . . .'

The young girl yielded adroitly. But others, his friends and colleagues, were not to yield, and he was to regard them as enemies. Violently broken friendships are like milestones in his life. Whatever Jones may say, his autotherapy did nothing to change this. And the proof recurs frequently in Jones' biography; for example he tells how Freud, in 1912, reproached Jung for not quoting his name often enough, and how he reacted to the resistance of the Swiss scholar by fainting (FLW, page 348). This obsession with a priority claim is expressed in the most astonishing way in various confidential remarks that he made to Fliess: 'Moebius is the best brain among the neurologists; luckily he has not stumbled on sexuality' (FFL, page 111). 'It was with a beating heart that I picked up Janet's *Hystérie et Idées fixes:* I put the book down with a calm pulse, he has not the key' (FFL, page 263). In the course of the misunderstandings and struggles which, later, led to the secession of famous psycho-analysts, Freud often refused to admit that others had come upon an idea before he had. One of the incidents that preceded the ending of his friendship with Fliess foreshadows conflicts to come: in 1900, during that meeting which was to be the last "congress" of the two friends, Freud revealed to Fliess that his last great discovery was bisexuality, and he quite refused to admit that he had got this idea from his friend who had expressed it to him repeatedly over a period of three years. The psychologist needed one week in order to perceive that he had been the victim of an amnesia all the stranger because he had already spoken very frequently of bisexuality in his letters, and had always quoted his friend when so doing.

MAN THE OBSTACLE TO MAN

So what Freud discovered in his auto-analysis was not the Oedipus Complex. It was, on the one hand, the continued existence, often unrealised, of what has been lived through, and the presence of a past which creates the tendency to reproduce certain infantile relationships—a discovery far from new, but one to which he was the first to give the place it deserves in any explanatory scheme. And, on the other hand, he discovered the possibility of exploring dreams as the most authentic expression of the entire man, of his conscious as of his unconscious. Although the study of dreams is a very ancient practice, we must recognise *Traumdeutung* as one of the most original and most fertile contributions made to modern psychology. Freud only read the numerous works devoted to dreams after having formulated his own theory—here he really did not need any predecessors.[1]

In *Traumdeutung* all the elements of a great creation are visible. The presence of the author is constantly felt, even when he is not writing about his own dreams. The double nature of psychology, which is simultaneously a science and a philosophic art, is apparent. Each interpretation shows itself to be a structural building up of elements dispersed in time and space, a selection and tendentious condensation which unite the discovered significance with the imagined significance.

If Freud intended to prove that dreams have at all times the

[1] On the other hand his friends, like his adversaries, had too easily failed to see what he had owed in almost every aspect of his psycho-analysis to his predecessors and contemporaries, notably to Herbart, author of a great number of fundamental concepts of which Freud was to make use (among others the principle of pleasure and repression); and to E. von Hartmann and even more so to Griesinger who from 1867 on ascribed, in his psychiatry, a far greater importance to the unconscious than to the contents of the conscious; to Meynert with his theory of the two egos and of inhibitions; to Breuer, Charcot, Forel, Lips, Fliess and Janet, among others. And later to Bleuler, Jung and Adler. If Freud was in the beginning misunderstood and absurdly underestimated by his colleagues, he was later to be over-estimated by those who, knowing psychology only through his writings, considered him as the prime source and author of all great discoveries.

function of wish-fulfilment (*Wunscherfüllung*), he did not ask
that they prove the permanence of the Oedipus Complex or of
incestuous desires. Nevertheless one characteristic is common to
all these dreams, to his own as to those of his patients; an inexorable jealousy, accompanied by a wish to root out the competitor
once and for all, and a feeling of resentment which forgives
nothing. Even ambition, which recurs so frequently in Freud's
dreams, is not defined solely in terms of an objective, but far
more often as a function of that envy which is inspired by a more
fortunate competitor and, generally speaking, by all those who
seem to be successful. Indeed throughout all the immense casuistry
of orthodox psycho-analysis, the incestuous fixation is rarely
expressed in terms of a real attachment, but almost always as a
more or less murderous desire directed against a third person who
is never far away. This is easily explained: the neurotic is as
incapable of loving as he is of renouncing the love that he expects
from others. According to his reckoning, that which he receives is
accounted to a god-like scale, while that which he himself has to
offer must be accounted according to the scale of a beggar who, in
giving very little, has given his all. The lesson to be learned from
all the dreams interpreted by Freud is that man is an obstacle to
man. If he cannot eliminate him by transforming him into an
amorous slave, then he must kill him. The person who does not
love me must die! The person who is loved by another (who
should be loving me) must also die!

Unlike psycho-analysis and vulgar psychology, the Adlerian
theory considers neurotic jealousy not as the expression of a
love, of a frustrated libidinous fixation, but as a manifestation
of the will to power and to domination. A man does not kill the
thing he loves, but sometimes he will kill that which he desires
to possess without being able to justify such possession by love.
Sadism in all its manifestations is the impotence to love fleeing
furiously from itself. Love being a relationship in which fraudulent sentiments are very quickly unmasked, swindlers here bring
more artifice into play than in any other situation in which human
qualities are put to the proof. That is why the neurotic hides and
betrays his deficiencies in love and in friendship above all others.

OEDIPUS AND JOSEPH

If Freud was not Oedipus in his memories of childhood, no more was he in his dreams; he was Joseph and aware of the fact, the son of Jacob's second wife, for long the youngest son and his father's favourite; the dreamer who sees his brothers bowing down before him, the sun, the moon and stars (his father, his mother and their children) making obeisance to him; Joseph who in a foreign country achieves power thanks to his art in divining dreams; the chaste man, exposed to female seduction, but who does not marry until he reaches the age of thirty; he is Joseph, mortally threatened by the envy and jealousy of his brothers.

Freud knowingly identified himself with Joseph, but he wished to discover in the Oedipus legend the fundamental parable of man, thus reducing the struggle of the generations, of the sexes, of the classes, and the struggle of man with his destiny, to the incestuous desire—and the revolt against oppressive authority to parricidal jealousy.

The background of the Greek tragedy is the story of the scandalous goings-on of the pensionaries on Mount Olympus and of those humans whose crimes were committed in a period when, willingly or not, they were inevitably involved in the divine orgies and the divine quarrels. The central fact of all tragedy is the punishment inflicted by gods on men.

Oedipus would never have killed his father if that father had not broken the links of vital solidarity existing between the generations. And Laios, whose keenest desire was to have a son, permitted in the most cowardly fashion that that son be put to death because he had been warned of the fate that the gods were preparing for him at the hands of the boy-baby. It is thus a tragedy of a consciousness whose every action helps, instead of hindering, the fulfilment of a terrible destiny. What the Sophoclean tragedy teaches is that moderation alone offers protection against the gods: every break in the solidarity that holds men together is of profit to the gods in the pursuit of their intrigues and their revenge. 'Do not kill, for your victim may be your father or your brother!' Every immoderate act produces a chain reaction in further acts of violence, becoming more and more terrible, to infinity. No man is truly a stranger, no goa is truly a friend.

It is obvious that this deed of Oedipus owes nothing to the complex named after him. There is, on the other hand, a deep affinity between the legend of Joseph and that of Oedipus. One like the other is first of all driven abroad. They are intruders and, as strangers, achieve the height of power, thereby saving their new country or their family broken asunder. Joseph recognises his brothers and humiliates them, but without destroying them; Oedipus fails to recognise his mother or his father, and that is why he must assume the guilt of his misdeeds. Incest is not here the result of a libidinous fixation, but quite the contrary, of a complete alienation, of the absence of those natural relationships which should have linked Jocasta and her son, had she accepted her destiny instead of trying to avoid it through an inhuman act of denial.

Let us nevertheless remember this; life being less dramatic than literature, long after his death Oedipus was to become the hero-protector of Attica, just as Joseph had been the protector of his people in his life-time.

The attraction exercised by the Oedipus legend on Freud, badly and trivially though he interpreted it, can be explained on at least four different levels: 1. All the determining factors are well concealed and must be uncovered if the action is to become comprehensible. The *other*, inherent in magic as in all mysticism, is here constantly present, whereas this is not to be found in the monotheist legend. 2. The sexual theme is implicit in the form of an unconsciously incestuous marriage. 3. Murderous violence is loosed within a family. 4. Every act is simultaneously crime and punishment. Expiation remains ineffective.

Now for Freud neurosis is precisely this: frustration the twin to satisfaction, sin and expiation, guilty desire and the sentiment of guilt. In the circle he travels, the neurotic is at least as much in pursuit of the Furies as they are in pursuit of him.

Freud's scheme of things ignores the historical society, and is only adapted to the patriarchal family. That is why Freud proclaimed over and over again that the Oedipus Complex was the central element (*Kernstück*) of his theory of neurosis. The family is the cauldron in which are boiled those overheated emotions that attach or oppose its members to one another. Whether psychic energy, in the form of the libido, assumes the form of love avid for possession or of hatred avid for murder, in either case the violence of frustrated desire becomes a desire for violence, ill kept in check by the action of the reality principle. And faced by a hostile world, all desires are resumed in one: the nostalgia for the lost paradise, the return to the womb which should never have been left. All extreme violence nourishes the nostalgia for nothingness.

We have good reason for thinking that incestuous relationships are far more common than could be guessed from a perusal of the law reports. Now in the psycho-analysist casuistry, although it is centred about incestuous desire, we never meet incest in practice. On the other hand the feeling of guilt in those who do practice it is neither more marked nor more grave than in perverts. The fear of being disgraced in the eyes of neighbours and of being punished by the law is real enough, but there is no tragic terror. (Sexual relationships between brother and sister are more frequent in the higher social classes and those between father and daughter in the poorer, notably in certain remote districts such as mountain villages where endogamy is, in any case, inevitable.)

Parricide is not a particularly rare phenomenon. The man who kills his father will usually defend his act by the same system of auto-justification that is invoked in any other sort of passionate murder. Persons who commit incest or parricide are usually as subject to repressions and inhibitions as are other neurotics. This is hardly surprising, since the persistence of a fixation directed towards a parent can generally be explained far more in terms of a fear of the future and of a psychic incapacity to create a new relationship, than of a very strong attachment to the past. Whatever the strength of such an attachment may be, man by his nature looks to the future, and his actions are inserted into a scheme of things whereby causality is coupled with finality.

Freud, recognising this finality at all points, misunderstood it nonetheless, and this for two reasons. In the first place, due to the mechanistic materialism of his early teachers, he conceived psychology to be a natural science, comparable to physics, strictly causalist, *voraussetzungslos und wertungsfrei*, that is to say without any basis other than that of facts verified by exact methods and existing outside the boundaries of any system of values. Later, like any other man whose life has been punctuated by a series of breaks, Freud became obsessed by a past that he had failed to absorb, and impregnated with the certainty that if God were dead, nevertheless his threats to sinners remained very much alive. Mechanistic determinism satisfied a need within him: man, the object of his own past as much as of that of his family, could never in any circumstances transform himself into the subject of his own future.

THE MYTHOLOGY OF THE GUILTY CONSCIENCE

Psycho-analysis became as a result a theory of man guilty both of that which he does and of that which he desires, guilty of an original sin committed afresh by each generation; it is a mythology of the evil conscience far more than a psychology of the unconscious; beneath its disguise as an energy theory we recognise again a demonology of the instincts which here play exactly the same part that the Jewish mystics of the Middle Ages attributed to *Yetzer harah*, to evil desire. (Only simple-minded persons will be astonished by the facility with which a harmony can be established between religious and agnostic determinisms. The former begins with the crushing of man's humanity, the latter ends therewith.)

Freud put a part of the Old Testament to psychology, as a man puts a poem to music. In his work we see again the appallingly 'jealous God' together with his spirit of vengeance and the guilt of man; but in Freud the great reconciliation promised by the prophets is omitted, to be replaced by that curse, that malediction, which decides destiny in the tragic stories of the Greeks, and of which the Christian church made, in the name of original sin, the basis and the justification of its practical morality.

Thus Freud, born twelve years after Nietzsche and dying thirty-nine years after that philosopher, remained the prisoner of a morality from which Nietzsche had already plucked most of the disguises, particularly the feeling of guilt, that sly and hypocritical false conscience. Freud gave a mechanistic, a 'scientific' terminology to the age-old premises of current morality: it is dangerous to play tricks with love, or for that matter with any of the instincts, which, driven away at a trot, come back at full gallop; everything has to be paid for here on earth; spiritual energy may be transformed, but it cannot disappear. The only sort of man he was prepared to know was the family man, man in reaction, thus neglecting not only man as a 'sociable' being but also man in solitude, man engaged in creative activity or faced with death. That is why, after a world war, he could explain the existence of modern armies by a libidinous fixation that the soldiers had towards their leader, and the great political movements by the homosexual 'component' of their adherents; all of which is scarcely more absurd than explaining the value and the effect of a work of art by the Oedipus Complex of the artist.

Later, partly abandoning the pleasure principle, he returned towards the aggression instinct which, since 1908, Alfred Adler had opposed to the libidinous impulses. By that time it was no longer a question merely of understanding those murders of which neurotics had only dreamed, but real assassinations undertaken with a view to exterminating entire peoples. Towards the end of his days the founder of psycho-analysis must have suspected that the language of family life is scarcely suitable for this dialogue with death: a dialogue from which life can only emerge permanently humiliated, and which the living can never break off, but which they can only survive, marked with a sign which resembles the wound of Abel as much as it does the mark of Cain. He also seems to have suspected that anguish might perhaps be something more than the effect of *coitus interruptus* or the expression of a guilt. Nevertheless, in an interview with Arthur Koestler a few months before his death, the aged exile thought to detect the reason for the crimes of the Nazis in their feeling of guilt. This is almost the same opinion as that which the Hassidic Rabbis of

Galicia used to advance to their flocks in an attempt to make them understand the deeper sense of the massacre of which they were about to be the victims. It is as though the long road travelled by the son of Jacob Freud, the Jew of Buczacz, had after many turnings led back to its starting point . . .

Sigmund Freud might think to have freed himself of religion because he had broken with it at a very early age. But a break is not a liberation; it can only be an enfranchisement and one that is seldom complete. Freud is great wherever and whenever he is destructive, but he is almost insignificant whenever he abandons the antithetical attitude; he had the perspicacity of a genius when attacking that laziness which regards as nonsense everything it fails to understand; and he showed himself the victim of a really appalling lack of awareness when, blind to his own 'system of tendentious perception' (Adler), he would reduce the condition of mankind to the accidents inherent in their instincts, the tragedies of Oedipus and Hamlet to incidents provoked by their incestuous desires, or the story of the emperor without his clothes (whose robes everybody admired except one child), to an exhibitionistic desire. It is beyond doubt that by 1885 it was high time the psychologist should make his way into the bedroom. But there was no need for him to confound it with the universe. Certainly in order to create a symbol it is often necessary to take the part for the whole, but in order to achieve comprehension no man is ever justified in reducing the whole to one of its parts. The facts about man, because they deal with a being in a state of development or becoming, cannot be reduced to their component parts; their immense variety is not accidental, but is of their very being, and is composed of that which man develops out of himself and of that which he adds to his being, whether real or fictional. Human nature cannot be simplified.

That great citizen of Vienna, Karl Kraus, made a joke when he said that psycho-analysis is an illness which pretends to be its own cure. He might have added that the same applies to every form of magic, to every religion and to every philosophy. And, speaking generally, to everything which, dealing with man, would be final and certain.

'Man is thus nothing but diguise, nothing but lies and hypocrisy, both towards himself and towards others,' Pascal said—an exaggeration, because Pascal was, particularly at that time, occupied with his own salvation. But it is of little importance how human beings be described, since the real question, according to Alfred Adler, is to know what human beings will become; what they will make of themselves and according to which pattern they will arrange their past, that raw material which conditions but does not determine their future. The cardinal significance that man ascribes to his past and all his secrets is summed up in the image which he makes of his future.

October 1954

FALSE SITUATIONS

T. E. Lawrence and his Two Legends

False Situations *1*

When a man of mature age, having at last escaped from the enclosure of his own pretence, looks at his past, in those hours which Hegel ascribed to Minerva, he is always overwhelmed by the certitude that in serious matters he has never been deceived by anybody save himself. And he is astonished by the artifices he has employed on each such occasion to silence the warnings of his own conscience. No doubt there are professional crooks, but, except in the lives of fools, their crookery does not affect others except insofar as it touches on the comedy of life. Imposture will never suffice to explain errors made in the really decisive choices: the choice of a wife, of a friend, or of a cause to which a man is prepared to devote his life. It is only after a rupture that we recognise those objections which, in fact, we had known even before we embarked on a particular course of action. We were not blinded, we simply closed our eyes, preferring a vision to the real aspect, a myth to the truth.

To the different explanations offered by psychology for each particular preference in each particular case, one general reason may be added: vision is more complete than sight, myth is never so fragmentary as truth. The truth shows up the contradictions, while the myth conceals them after having first reconciled them.

The rationalists of the last century were convinced that once God had been abolished the myths and legends would simultaneously disappear, along with every sort of superstition. But our age has created a hundred new Mounts Olympus, which it peoples inexhaustibly with demi-gods whose diverse natures satisfy every taste and fulfil every dream: war heroes, boxers, film stars, supermen, scientists, saviours of their people, breakers of athletic records, adventurers with metaphysical pretensions. Humanity today, repeatedly achieving what was yesterday regarded as impossible, thus finds the nourishment for its imagination which remains eternally starved. Despite all technical development, man can still digest only a very small part of that which he sees. The rest is lost, remaining unknown, not understood; this is the fog that envelops his consciousness. In the practical matters of daily life his experience, mutilated though it be, more or less suffices for his needs; but in other matters he will call in the assistance of myths and of rediscovered legends, to show him the way and to help him adjust to the society in which he lives.

Heads can be crammed with nonsense. This was done most effectively during the First World War, but this 'filling of a void' is as old as humanity itself. What on the other hand appears relatively new, is the way that so many intellectuals have taken a hand in it, the frantic enthusiasm with which they have set about inventing those lamps which, according to the poet Christian Morgenstern, disseminate darkness everywhere as soon as they are lit. It used to be said that when soothsayers met they smiled at one another—they might deceive others but could not deceive themselves. Our contemporary soothsayers, however, are inclined even to believe in their own rubbish.

Richard Aldington, novelist, poet and essayist, recently took up arms against what he considers to be an entirely fabricated legend. He decided to destroy it once and for all by means of one book: *Lawrence of Arabia, a Biographical Enquiry.* (The French edition of this book has a thoroughly aggressive title: *Lawrence l'imposteur.*) The critics, both English and French, have generally condemned this destructive biography and have reproached the author for his exasperated nagging and his puritanical meanness; but they have hardly destroyed the conclusions that his zealous 'researches' have allowed him to draw. He denounces lies, reveals tendentious exaggerations, abusive glorifications, the subtilisation of obvious facts. Yet nevertheless he fails in what he tries to do: he has not succeeded in destroying the legend, because he conceives of it as a tissue of counter-truths built upon half-truths, whereas in fact it is rather a mixture of that 'fiction' which is subjective truth and of those errors which can seduce more easily than truth can convince.

If the legend of Lawrence of Arabia is an imposture, its hero was its only victim. The price he paid was that of unspeakable suffering. The author of *Death of a Hero* seems to have suspected this, but he refuses to allow himself the least twinge of sympathy, of pity for T. E. Lawrence, that man cruelly tortured by what was simultaneously the best and the worst in himself.

More than twenty years have passed since his death. His case today remains as rich in instruction as ever it was, for it is not simply concerned with Lawrence but with an age, his age and ours, and with truly astonishing aberrations, both his and ours.

2

Thomas Edward, the second of the five sons born to Robert Thomas and to Sara Lawrence, came into this world on the 16th of August 1888. He often pretended that he was born one day earlier—as did Napoleon. (It was probably on his suggestion that one of his biographers attempted to establish an analogy between the fateful dates in the life of the Emperor and in that of the 'uncrowned king'.) Aldington was the first person to reveal Lawrence's genealogy to the public. However it had long been known in certain circles that his family story was a complicated one. Henceforth it seems established that R. T. Lawrence was in reality an Anglo-Irish baronet by the name of Chapman, who had married and become the father of four daughters before his union with the hospital nurse, Sara Junner.

While preserving the manners and the very pronounced tastes of a gentleman of his class, Lawrence's father had sunk both socially and financially, doubtless because of his love for the young Scottish woman, a rigid Calvinist whose strong personality seems to have impressed everyone who came in contact with her. (When a widow, she became a missionary in China at the age of sixty.) The Chapman family refused to recognise this union, and the children sprung from it, even after one of these had achieved glory.

According to a letter that he wrote to Mrs Bernard Shaw, his close friend, it was at the age of ten that Lawrence first learned the truth about his family's ambiguous situation. Aldington, who has read this letter, tends to believe that it was only seven years later that Lawrence first became aware of the 'sin', and consequent loss of status, of his parents. He experienced a sensation of shame which was to remain with him all his life. It is a fact that Lawrence gave his successive biographers very different stories concerning his genealogy, all equally remote from the truth. Did he wish to conceal this for his mother's sake? If this be the explanation, he set about doing so in a particularly maladroit fashion.

No psychologist would dare evaluate the importance that this discovery may have had in the formation of Lawrence's character. What is striking is that, throughout his life, Lawrence was to find himself involved in false situations; he entered them, fled from them, recreated them. 'False situations': no title would better suit his writings if they were all to be collected together in one volume.

After frequent changes of address, his family finally settled down at Oxford. It was here that Lawrence spent his youth. Later he often returned. He never rid himself of a mannered way of speaking, nor of certain 'tics' and exaggerated modes of expression, which, in the eyes of Englishmen, seem to characterise Oxford men.

The child seems to have been gifted, but not extraordinarily so; his intelligence was acute, he showed a great curiosity for technical matters as well as for everything that could nourish his very active imagination, a passion for reading, and an inexhaustible interest, which was relatively precocious, for relics of the past and notably of the Middle Ages. He was to say later that objects had always attracted him far more than ideas.

He enjoyed sport, but did not take part in team games such as football or cricket, and this inevitably cut him off from his contemporaries. He then developed a technique to protect his individuality, and assumed a position of ironical superiority. Thus he would wait, day after day, beside the school gate for his fellow pupils to come out, and would follow them solemnly to the football field in order to explain to them after their game 'their qualities and defects considered according to the Hellenic criterion of the perfection of the body.' This anecdote reflects quite well the attitude of the solitary person, who tends to over-compensate for a feeling of inferiority by setting himself up as the judge of those whose society he flees for fear lest he fail to prove himself their equal.

Lawrence stopped growing too early. The fact that he was shorter than the average Englishman never ceased to worry him, and seems to have determined certain aspects of this tendency to devalue others, as it did his sense of humour which its victims described as 'impish'.

His own body remained one of his dominant preoccupations until his death. Even as an adolescent he made it his victim, and never ceased to compel it to submit to a will which grew constantly more capricious and cruel. He forbade it the joys and satisfactions of love, and loved it with an often contemptuous and always exacting severity. But this had nothing in common with the practices of those saints who would force their senses into silence.

From his early youth Lawrence enslaved his own body—the principal instrument by which he would realise his 'fiction'. During four summers (1906, 1907, 1908, 1910), he travelled across France, studying the mediaeval castles and the pottery of that country, often bicycling sixty miles or more a day, usually entirely alone. He travelled in Syria and once in Mesopotamia, on foot, exposing himself to dangers as real as they were pointless, imposing upon his highly sensitive body feats of endurance, compelling it to submit to circumstances which never failed to provoke within him the most intolerable sensations of disgust. (Even later, he could never see a reptile without a shudder of horror, and he forced himself to go barefoot.) Turning upon this ill-loved body of his which was always to remain that of an adolescent, he conquered it daily in a struggle made all the more inevitable owing to the 'fiction' through which he observed it.

It is impossible to establish the exact moment at which he began this violent dialogue with the tangible part of his being. It may

be imagined that it started after an accident that kept him im-
mobilised for several months with a broken ankle. But why should
this incident have produced such an effect? Any answer can only
be hypothesis.

Under the influence of a puritanical education he may have
first considered his body as the incarnation of sin, but at the age
of seventeen he lost his faith. That same year Lawrence met the
man who was to become for him, in his own words, 'the parent
I could trust, without qualification, to understand what bothered
me ... the only person to whom I never had to explain the 'why'
of what I was doing.' [1] David G. Hogarth (1862-1927) was an
archaeologist, specialising in the civilisations of the Near East,
who had been in charge of excavations carried out in Egypt, on
Cyprus, at Ephesus, in Crete and at Carchemish. An unusual
scholar, he had acquired a general reputation through the success
of his book: *A Wandering Scholar in the Levant.* Lawrence met
him at the Ashmolean Museum, of which Hogarth was the director.
Then in his forties, Hogarth must have recognised the extreme
sensitivity that this adolescent failed to conceal behind his
somewhat sneering manner and his pointlessly aggressive attitude.
Lawrence, lacking self-assurance, tended to throw the value of his
own singular personality into full relief; this did not prevent the
scholar from recognising in the young Lawrence that ability of
concentrating his entire attention and his entire strength upon
one objective which is characteristic of all gifted men. From that
moment, Hogarth had trust in him: he opened the road that was
to take him to Carchemish and, during the war, to Cairo and to
Arabia. (Hogarth was head of the Arab Bureau: it inspired the
policy that led the British to support the Arab revolt in the
Hedjaz.)

Before Lawrence's first departure for Syria, Hogarth introduced him to a great and famous old man: Charles M. Doughty,
the poet, who after travels in Arabia between 1876 and 1878 had
published his *Travels in Arabia Deserta*—an astonishing work,
the influence of which on Lawrence has almost completely

[1] *Selected Letters of T. E. Lawrence,* Cape, 1952, pp. 254 and 257. This
volume is henceforth referred to as 'Letters'.

escaped the attention of continental admirers of *The Seven Pillars of Wisdom*.

In 1910 Lawrence finished his thesis on the Crusaders' castles. He maintained that this form of military architecture was due to a western inspiration, which the Europeans had subsequently transported to Asia. In this he disagreed, and continued to disagree, with the majority of authorities, who ascribe an oriental origin to castles of this sort.

During these years in which Lawrence took part in excavations carried out on behalf of the British Museum, he proved himself to be a remarkably efficient man, particularly when it was a question of overcoming technical difficulties or of solving the problems which inevitably arise when dealing with native labour. His relationship with the Arabs was far more personal than were those of his colleagues. He became intimately attached to a young boy and a foreman whom he even brought back for a summer at Oxford. Thanks to his studies before setting off for his solitary excursions in the orient, he had learnt sufficient Arabic to be able to speak the language easily; his knowledge of it, however, remained largely empirical.

He sometimes admired the physique of the Arabs, laughed at their superstitions, was moderately interested in their picturesque dress, but showed very little interest in their religion or their folklore. He obviously did not regard it as his duty to help in their liberation, nor was he apparently interested in political matters.

What drew him closer to the native was the fact that he enjoyed dressing in their clothes. He gives quite unconvincing explanations for this tendency on his part; a tendency to be emphasised later, during the revolt in the desert, when he chose an Arabic costume white as snow and decorated in such a way as to show to all that he was the friend of Feisal: *Lurens*.

This peculiarity in choice of clothes, and even more his attempts to justify it, characterise fairly well the attitude which transpires in many other complicated undertakings of Lawrence's: his vanity was such that it forbade him—in vain as it happened—to be vain. In order to appear strikingly spectacular, he always had to have recourse to the subterfuges of that false modesty with which Socrates reproached the young Alcibiades. He despised this vanity of his in all sincerity, but, trying at least to conceal it, he only succeeded in making it all the more demanding. He became the man of the *redoubled pose,* the actor in a contrapuntal game.

His sense of humour led him to perform what are known as practical jokes; he was prepared to sacrifice everything in order to carry out a joke, in which the 'fiction' transformed into the reality fools spectators, who are thus doubly taken in: they go on believing that the joker is only spilling red ink, when in fact he is shedding real blood.

Despite their peculiarities, Lawrence's origins as well as his education (like those of the greater part of the English intelligentsia) placed him in a privileged social group, comparable to a junior nobility. Even today that intelligentsia remains loyal to its way of life, mantaining its pretensions despite a financial decline which is often total. It is in effect an aristocracy, usually without titles: or a club that is not a clique, and possesses no written code. Lawrence wished to belong to this group, but was never quite certain that he did so. His jokes revealed his painfully equivocal position: he wished to convince that he was always what he played at being, while he was never sure if the part in which he had cast himself was really what he had to be. He could adapt himself to any way of life whatsoever, because none seemed to him to be really his legitimate one; he could take on any part, attach himself to any sort of person, for he knew that in truth he would be linked with nobody, with nothing. When with Arabs or Englishmen, he was neither Arab nor English (nor for that matter Irish), remaining always and desperately himself, feeling now infinitely superior, now infinitely beneath his fellows.

On the invitation of Captain S. F. Newcombe, Lawrence and a colleague undertook researches on the Sinai Peninsula early in 1914. The purpose of these was to establish, for the benefit of the British Army, the topography of a region that might assume strategical importance in case of war, and to do this as fully as possible. Such a collaboration between archaeologists and the Intelligence Service doubtless amused Lawrence. Whatever his hagiographers may say, this undertaking in no way inspired the great projects which he was to attempt to realise during the World War.

He had just finished his report on *The Wilderness of Zin* when that war broke out. It is said that he wished to enlist, but that he was turned down on the grounds that he was not sufficiently tall. He was employed by the army as a civilian and later, in December of 1914, was sent to Cairo as a second lieutenant. He there worked in the Maps Department of the Army's Intelligence Service and also helped to collate incoming information concerning the disposition of Turkish forces in the Near East.

Lawrence thought that sooner or later England must clash with France, and this provided the basis for his few political ideas. He developed this thesis in his letters to D. Hogarth; the British must seize Alexandretta, for if this port were to become a French possession, France would be in a position to launch an expeditionary force of a hundred thousand men against the Suez Canal twelve days after a declaration of war. He insisted that Hogarth must try to convince Churchill of this, and pushed him with all his strength towards this end. Again and again his letters return to this proposed seizure of Alexandretta, underlining how vitally important it was that the French be prevented from establishing themselves in Syria. Idrisi, he hoped, would quickly capture Damascus and thus put an end to French ambitions.

Lawrence was unhappy in Cairo, a lonely figure among regular officers who regarded him as an oddity. He wished to escape, and hoped for a posting, with Newcombe, as adviser to Idrisi. But that Arab chieftain was eliminated, and this hope evaporated. In 1915 Hogarth arrived in Cairo and the Arab Bureau was installed there. Lawrence was not a member of the organisation, but continued to be in charge of the Arabic bulletin and went on serving as a map officer.

Thus two years went by. Great events were shaking the world, but the tumult of huge battles was only a distant, muffled din by the time it reached the Egyptian office where Lawrence performed the functions of a minor official: Lawrence who, in 1914, had decided that within four years at most, that is to say by the time he was thirty, he would have become a general and would have been ennobled. Yet he was still only a subaltern, and one ill-adjusted to his environment. His contemporaries were fighting in France and dying in Flanders; two of his brothers had already been killed in action. History, bloody and outrageous, was daily pursuing its stupid course; each day Lawrence, behind his desk, corrected the spelling of difficult Arab place names. But since, despite everything, he remained a member of the 'club' and since, doubtless thanks to Hogarth, he was well-informed about what was going on, he was able to judge the incompetence of those soldiers who, visibly, understood nothing about a war where all the certainties on which they had based the principles of their art were being proved wrong. The infantryman's entrenching tool had proved to be an invincible weapon. On the French front where the outcome of this first world conflict was being decided, the generals were showing an ingenuity of mind and an adaptability to circumstances that would scarcely have done credit to a tug-of-war team. As our twentieth century began, their murderous incapacity was transforming Europe's youth into cannon fodder.

With the ironical eye of the dilettante enslaved to no tradition and to no sanctified prejudice, the young historian observed the arrogant world of those experts who were so grossly ignorant in the one field where they pretended to be absolute masters. To the freedom of the solitary man, he added the feeling of his own intellectual superiority over the majority of these 'men of destiny' and the certainty that he was not their accomplice, that he had no responsibility whatsoever for their undertakings in which men were being pointlessly killed. It is possible, though scarcely probable, that it was at this time that Lawrence began to think it was up to dilettantes such as himself to put an end to the disorder created by the military specialists, and to conceive of a strategy which would once again restore mobility to warfare, and with it the element of surprise. (Of his contemporaries two other dilettantes conceived similar ideas, Winston Churchill and Leon Trotsky.)

But it scarcely mattered what Lawrence thought about this

war: his position was insignificant, his situation that of a civilian disguised as a soldier, billeted in Cairo where operations were being directed upon a front of minimum importance. The Gallipoli expedition had failed; on the other hand the Turkish threat to Suez no longer existed; the British forces had been defeated outside Ghaza and had been compelled to surrender in humiliating circumstances in Mesopotamia. The Ottoman Empire, that 'sick man of Europe', was proving a remarkably sturdy invalid, an extremely formidable enemy on the defensive, if less so when attacking.

The British were inclined to pay a high price for an auxiliary army, and to make vast promises to any Arab movement likely to provoke and maintain a revolt that would compel the Turks to disperse, at least in part, their military forces. The Turks had only small numbers of men available for the defence of Syria and Arabia, but England, whose sons were dying in Europe, was scarcely in a position to assemble in the Middle East an army markedly superior in strength to that of her adversaries; and without such an army she hesitated, as is her custom, to try and force the decision. Meanwhile she knew by her long experience that there were other courses of action which might produce at least limited results; throughout the centuries, wherever she has not herself held power, England has known how to derive profit from the nationalism of oppressed peoples by encouraging their boldest dreams. This community of interests, linking the British with nationalist movements determined to destroy the empires of others, has always conjured up allies for the United Kingdom, allies who, impotent without her, must submit to her will before they can proclaim their own independence.

In appealing to Arab nationalism, the British knew how it could serve their cause, but they were unaware of its real meaning: there did not then exist any Arab nation which could be selected as the unifying element. In addition to Syria, a geographical term both artificial and lacking in precision, there was Mesopotamia, the tribes of the Hedjaz, of Nedjd and many others. Where was the movement to be centred? Who would be set up as its leader? Nationalism was most outspoken in the towns, such as Damascus and Beirut—the French had effectively contributed to this—but the moment war broke out the Turkish administrators in those cities had succeeded in decapitating the movement. On the other hand it was as well to avoid stirring up Mesopotamia; popular uproars close to oil wells are never particularly desirable. Ibn Saud, in the Nedjd, was an ally, but of too independent a nature; he fought when and how he wished. There remained the Hedjaz, adjoining the Red Sea, with as prince the Sheik Hussein and his ambitious sons who had been brought up at the court of Istanbul. The Arab Bureau, an agency of the Foreign Office, examined the possibilities here. An agreement was made with Hussein, and the date was fixed on which he was to launch a rebellion against the scattered Turkish garrisons and seize control of the principal towns of his sheikdom. The revolt, breaking out before the agreed date, was moderately successful, but failed at Medina, the terminus of the railway line. (The Turks were in fact not to abandon this town until four months after the end of the war.)

There was no fear of a Turkish offensive, for British naval supremacy ruled out any action based on the Arab ports and directed against Egypt, while the desert was hardly likely to attract the Turks, involving as it would an enormous dispersal of their strength. On the other hand, allied strategy had a considerable interest in ensuring at least the neutrality of the tribes of the Hedjaz and even more so those of the Sinai Peninsula, who would find themselves upon the right flank of any allied army attacking in a general easterly direction. Furthermore, any action against the Hedjaz line which might permanently cut the lines of communication linking the twenty thousand Turks in Medina with the north was highly desirable. The normal activity of most of these tribes went by the name of *rezzous,* skirmishes that they fought between themselves on different pretexts of which the vendetta remained their favoured *casus belli,* but sometimes taking the form of attacks on pilgrims and on trains. Thus the British had first to establish a truce between the tribes; and to do this they had to compensate them for the loss that they would suffer, at least provisionally, in unacquired booty. British gold served to convince the most stubborn of the tribes. Another

effective argument, when spread among the tents, was rumours
of the miraculous loot to be captured by *rezzous* against the
trains. The thunder of European explosions seemed to the sons of
the desert to promise a deluge of gold. French and British officers
led these destructive expeditions, living with the Bedouin,
flattering them, buying and advising their leaders.

Lawrence was one of these, arriving relatively late upon the
scene, and was not among the most effective in these destructive
undertakings. Colonel Storrs allowed Lawrence to accompany him
on one of his missions to the Sheik. This was in September of
1916, and by then the map officer was reaching the end of his
career in Egypt, for his situation had become untenable. When he
set off for a few weeks' journey, all that he could hope to find on
his return was a job with the Arab Bureau, thanks to a word
from Hogarth.

Hussein, who had no wish to leave Mecca, let them listen by
telephone to music played by a Turkish military band that his
son Abdulla had captured in a skilful and lucky ambush. It was
neither in the course of these conversations with Abdulla, nor on
the occasion of his meeting with Ali, the Sheik's eldest son, that
Lawrence first visualised all that the revolt might become.
Before returning to Cairo he visited the camp of Feisal, Hussein's
third son. 'Framed between the uprights of a black doorway,
stood a white figure waiting tensely for me. I felt at first glance
that this was the man I had come to Arabia to seek—the leader
who would bring the Arab Revolt to full glory. Feisal looked
very tall and pillar-like, very slender, in his long white silk robes.'

These words that Lawrence wrote five years later show the
myth in all its glory. He has already told the readers of *The Seven
Pillars of Wisdom* the circumstances in which he had undertaken
this journey, and what were his intentions on his return to
Egypt—it is obvious that he did not in fact go into the Hedjaz
looking for someone. The fiction is thus retroactive, though it is
not a lie, as Aldington claims. He was obeying the necessity of
his style, which is almost Victorian in its pure sublimity. And this,
incidentally, allows him not to reveal what it was that showed
him at first glance that Feisal must be the leader. That style is

maintained even to the obvious question that the young sheik put to him: 'And do you like our place here?' And to his reply: 'Well; but it is far from Damascus.' And he adds, in his book: 'The word had fallen like a sword in their midst. There was a quiver. Then everybody stiffened where he sat, and held his breath for a silent minute.'

The report of these conversations, submitted by Lawrence to his superior officers as soon as he was back in Cairo, impressed the generals, doubtless because of its intrinsic interest, but also because the conclusions that he drew confirmed their own opinion: there was no need to send British troops into Arabia. Arab soldiers under the orders of their sheiks (advised by British officers) would suffice for the task, once they had received material aid in the form of guns and gold. If they were provided with the tools they would repay their debt by winning the victory. It was decided to send the author of this comforting report as an adviser to Feisal.

Attached at last to the Arab Bureau and promoted Captain, Lawrence set off on his mission. His powers were limited in the extreme and, what is more, somewhat ill-defined, as was usually the case with those political agents dressed in military uniforms and to be seen almost everywhere by the side of native chieftains—chieftains whose ambitions were always revealed as grossly exaggerated, while their courage in action often appeared to be remarkably limited. Others gave and carried out the orders; Lawrence's determination was to try and inspire those orders. For the first time in his life he saw the reality verging towards the 'fiction', that is to say towards the deepest and most secret part of his own being. He entered into this revolt of others as though they were but actors destined to play parts in his own dream.

He wrote an account of what he lived through, undertook, hoped and suffered during those two years which were to create his legend, and he called his book: *The Seven Pillars of Wisdom— a triumph.* This book is of a very moving sincerity whenever, fleeing his own past, he is telling his story to himself; when he is writing with an eye on those who, in this mirror, will search for confirmation that their hero is worthy of their adulation, it is one of redoubled poses that astonish by their constant self-contradiction.

In this tale, one of the greatest of our century, an attentive reader will find many more arguments to destroy the myth than are advanced by Aldington in his *Life of Lawrence;* but at the same time he will find every reason for admiring a writer whose weaknesses increase instead of diminishing his stature, a book which only becomes dubious, sometimes even ridiculous, in those passages where Lawrence, victim of the mythomania of his admirers, postures as the master of an historic destiny.

We know what it was that Lawrence did in Arabia. From the point of view of a man who fought on the Western front—as did Aldington—it is not particularly remarkable. We know what he suffered. Compared to the sufferings at Verdun it was really very little. We know the ruses that he employed in order to achieve certain relatively important ends in a guerilla war where distances were the only obstacles, and that he won his victories in places where there was usually no enemy.

The Bedouin in the Arabian desert, like the *guerilleros* in Spain a century earlier and the partisans led by Kutusov in Russia, did not look for battle, but for the effects of surprise. Lawrence needed to invent nothing, but only to apply the lesson learned from experiences that were generally known. The hopes that he had based upon an Arab army of liberation soon vanished. He recognised that it would be impossible really to make war against the Turks and to dislodge them from Medina, and folly to launch a frontal attack. In order to seize places such as Wejh or Akaba, it was a question of mobilising (by buying) the tribes living nearest to those places. For he was always dealing with tribes and their leaders, and not with an Arab nation (which did not exist), nor with a national army.

The only battle which he was prepared to fight, which he arranged, and in which he commanded, was a skirmish at Tafileh. He has described it in detail: a bloody and stupid choreography, as are all battles large or small, mounted by dilettantes whose intellectual processes on this occasion reached the level of the tricks used by boy scouts playing in the woods. In describing this battle Lawrence, deliberately no doubt, modelled his account on that which Tolstoi gives of the Battle of Borodino, a piece of prose he is known to have admired greatly. At Tafileh he postures simultaneously as Napoleon and as Kutusov, but he manages to take himself seriously when describing the quite unnecessary sufferings which he forced himself to undergo. Until the very end of his life he was to continue to believe in that type of voluntary sacrifice where the victim is both his own god and his own executioner.

There is nothing sublime about battle: it is one immense practical joke, which humiliates the combatants whom it does not kill. And victory? For the archaeologist, that which separates victors from vanquished is a thin layer of earth in the vertical cut; the remnants of the cities of the conquerors are uncovered a few days, sometimes only a few hours, before the cities of those whom they conquered. Only the soil is victorious, entombing with indifference the victors and their unfortunate victims alike. Lawrence knew this. Nevertheless he believed in victory, and passionately desired it. When at last he entered Damascus he realised that the triumph was not his, that in fact his fantasy had faded away the moment that he left the desert. He obtained permission from Allenby to go away. 'And then at once I knew how much I was sorry.' Those are the last words of the last chapter of his great book. They are followed by a brief epilogue of which the two first paragraphs run:

'Damascus had not seemed a sheath for my sword, when I landed in Arabia; but its capture disclosed the exhaustion of my main springs of action. The strongest motive throughout had been a personal one, not mentioned here, but present to me, I think, every hour of these two years. Active pains and joys might fling up, like towers, among my days: but, refluent as air, this hidden urge re-formed, to be the persisting element of life, till near the end. It was dead, before we reached Damascus.

'Next in force had been a pugnacious wish to win the war: yoked to the conviction that without Arab help England could not pay the price of winning its Turkish sector. When Damascus fell, the Eastern war—probably the whole war—drew to an end.'

In the first paragraph all is enigma, and like the poem which serves as apologue to his book, must confuse the reader who is prepared to insert the reality within the framework of the 'fiction' rather than extract the 'fiction' from the reality.

Let us first of all insist on one obvious fact. In order to act as he did, Lawrence had primarily the same motives as the few score British officers, political agents and others in the Middle East and the millions of men who, on other fronts, were engaged on occupations which would seem very strange did we not know that this was a question of a war fought by armies of conscripted men for fifty and one months. The question of personal motive which in the beginning no doubt exists for volunteers, rapidly disappears. Collective action is determined solely by the aim that is assigned to it.

The readers of an account dealing with some striking and dangerous undertaking, as for example the scaling of a mountain peak, do not expect their author to disclose his personal motives. They would be taken aback and somewhat irritated if one of these mountaineers were to add to his account of what he had done an epilogue in these terms: 'I am keeping one secret. I shall never tell you, no never, what was the extraordinary reason that led me to plant a flag on the summit of Annapurna.'

How then are we to explain the fact that Lawrence, writing three years after the end of the war, felt the need of telling us that there existed an unsuspected secret? Did he wish to mystify the reader, to worry him with the idea that after some seven hundred pages he still knew nothing about that 'I' to whom he had been listening, and who seemed to have kept nothing back? Was it the advance publicity for a second volume? Not at all. Lawrence simply felt that he must give an answer to a question that he himself had raised, by presenting this war as his war, as a personal adventure in which all the others engaged were simply so much raw material.

Having transformed the reality into an egotistical 'fiction', he then had to give a psychological interpretation of it. (Perhaps the expedition to climb Mount A can be explained in terms of a motive personal to mountaineer B, who, urged on by remorse, went there in search of the young girl whom he had dishonoured fifteen years before?)

The capture of Damascus, the raids carried out by the Arab tribes against the Turks, and so many other of the events described by Lawrence, would undoubtedly have taken place even if the young archaeologist had never once left Oxford between the years 1914 and 1918. 'When Damascus fell the Eastern war—probably the whole war—drew to an end.' Not at all. The war ended with the defeat of Germany, in the Balkans as much as in the Near East, and the Turkish troops thereupon threw away their arms on all the roads leading towards Damascus. There is no way of telling whether, without the desert Arabs, the entry of the Australian troops into the town would have been held up by so much as one single day. But it is certain that the Turks had lost, here as everywhere else, the day that the offensive led by Franchet d'Esperey crushed Bulgaria.

The epilogue adds:

'Then I was moved by curiosity. *Super flumina Babylonis*, read as a boy, had left me longing to feel myself the node of a national movement. We took Damascus, and I feared. More than three arbitrary days would have quickened in me a root of authority.

'There remained historical ambition, insubstantial as a motive by itself. I had dreamed, at the City School in Oxford, of hustling into form, while I lived, the new Asia which time was inexorably bringing upon us. Mecca was to lead to Damascus; Damascus to Anatolia, and afterwards to Bagdad; and then there was Yemen. Fantasies, these will seem, to such as are able to call my beginning an ordinary effort.'

In the bulky private papers of Lawrence and of his close friends there is nothing to show that he had ever expressed any desire to be at the centre of a national movement, whether in Ireland, in

Arabia or elsewhere. During his Syrian period, living in constant touch with the Arabs, he nowhere shows any interest in their national aspirations. And in 1915, as we have seen, he was worried by a French threat to the Suez canal, without thinking 'of hustling into form . . . the new Asia.'

Finally, there was no need for him to fear the awakening within himself of any lust for authority as the result of his exercise of power. What power? He had had power when dealing with Feisal or with Auda in his capacity as the representative of Great Britain. But face to face with the British Army, what did he represent at Damascus? Feisal? Feisal was sent for, in order that it might be decided what should be done with him. The Arab army? Where was it? The National Movement in Syria? It had its leaders and its spokesmen. Lawrence was obviously not of their number.

He was by this time thirty years old, the age by which he had decided that he would be a general and a nobleman. He was neither the one nor the other, but enriched by an experience which, disintegrating his past, threatened to alienate him from himself. Between October 1916 and October 1918 he had lived as though he were really the man whose part he had been playing. But apart from this game of make-believe, what was he? A young archaeologist who had lost four years of his life, as had all those millions of men now ripe for demobilisation who were about to return to civilian life and try to forget as quickly as possible the rôle that they had been compelled to play. But as for Lawrence, it was a rôle that he had chosen. Other British officers in the Desert had acted according to the orders that they had received, amateurs despite themselves in the affairs of Arabia. He alone had given himself to this business without reserve: he had there found his realisation.

Back in London, he continued to walk about in Arab costume. In the spring of 1919, in Paris where he acted as Feisal's interpreter, he was still an Arab. At this same period he embarked upon the pathetic game of guilty conscience: the British not having kept the promises that he had made in their name to the Arabs, that is to say to Hussein's family, he announced that he felt dishonoured. As often happens in those false yet sublime tragedies of which the only heroine is conscience (a bad conscience, obviously) it was here a question of a displacement or of a subtilisation, real but inadmissible, of the subject matter. We are reminded of the Italian prince who bitterly reproached himself for having murdered his adversaries now buried in his garden; walking up and down between their graves he wished to assure himself, without offending his code of morals, that they were really, once and for all eliminated. His remorse was nothing but cries of triumph.

The remorse of T. E. Lawrence expressed nothing save his pretensions to an exaggerated grandeur, inevitably lost. Furthermore, by April of 1919 at the latest, he knew that his views on the whole Arab situation had been fundamentally mistaken: the power of the Desert did not reside with the Hashemites, as he had thought. They were about to be quite easily crushed by the Wahabites, who are at the present time the uncontested masters of the Hedjaz as well as of the Nedjd.

Great Britain could not maintain Feisal upon the throne of Syria, because she did not succeed in imposing her own domination there. She did succeed in Iraq, and she invented the Kingdom of Transjordania in order to give Abdullah a throne. And what about the Arab revolt? It broke out at last, but when it did so it was directed against the rule of the Husseinites, whom it chased out of their own sheikdom.

If, ten months after the capture of Damascus, there was one expert on Arabic matters in England who knew for sure that all the mystique about the desert liberator of the Arabs was simply ridiculous and the strength of the Hashemites an absurd myth, that man was Lawrence (whose knowledge was only rivalled by that of Philby, the British representative with Ibn Saud).

It was at this time that the American journalist, Lowell Thomas, put on a show at Covent Garden, *The Prince of Mecca,* in all his glory, 8.30 each evening, matinées Wednesday, Thursday and Saturday at 2.30. Its success was immense. The intimate and unexpressed "fiction" of Lawrence now encountered the fantasy of the crowd: the legend of glory. He despised it while adoring it. It was all a farce in the worst possible taste, particularly coming as it did at the precise moment when he should have admitted that he had been unable to foresee anything whatsoever.

His decision one day to write his own *Arabia Deserta* was doubtless taken long before his adventures were over. He claims that he wrote the first draft of the *Seven Pillars* before August, 1919, and that he lost it (or it was stolen) in a railway station at about the end of this year. This is possible but scarcely probable. He says he wrote a second version which he finished in 1920 and burned after having used it as the basis for his third and final version, completed in February of 1922.

It may be presumed that the book which he had conceived in Arabia, and of which he had perhaps outlined certain chapters before his return to London in August of 1919, was entirely different from the one which he finally wrote. After that date—August 1919—he was never again to be alone, for his legend was to accompany him wherever he went. As a writer he could not but be aware that his book would inevitably be defined by its relationship with the legend of its author. He took a very serious decision: *The Seven Pillars of Wisdom* would destroy that legend and simultaneously the legendary hero, Colonel Lawrence.

But in this as in every other matter his decision was not complete. His book could not really burst asunder the glorious lie, since it would not be published; only a limited circle of persons chosen by himself would be allowed to read it. And Colonel Lawrence would not really die, but would simply disappear by changing his identity and by cutting himself off forever from his own past. The idea of a complete break with the past as a substitute for suicide is not a new one. The wish to deny once and for all one's own actions, to be finally rid of them, is frequently to be encountered in the dreams of those men who are still linked to life solely by the logic of their bodies, but who have no attachment with other beings: no attachment either in the form of what they have received nor even in what they have given. This dream is born of a solitude capable of destroying even the affection that a man has for himself.

Lawrence had thus decided to go away as soon as he should have finished his book, to slide into a way of life where he no longer could dispose of himself, to mark his failure by establishing himself at a level which, from both the human and the social aspect, would be the very lowest. He desired to be rid of the 'fiction' which he had lived (and not merely told, as Aldington believes). But behind this idea of flight there was already perceptible another 'fiction', an *imago* of melancholy grandeur: he would be a Haroun-al-Rashid renouncing forever splendours that he would never see again ... an outcast lost in a crowd of outcasts, he would keep the secret of his misunderstood majesty, but at the same time he would preserve the power of carrying out a transformation scene whenever he should so choose. But he would never so choose. Thus the little Dolgoruki boy, the adolescent of whom Dostoievsky wrote, humiliated by his illegitimate birth and his ironically high-sounding name, by his poverty and by a false situation from which there was no escape, dreamed of amassing an immense fortune in order to scatter it proudly before all the world.

Lawrence went away, slamming the door behind him, but he did not really close it. He made an agreement with an important figure in the R.A.F. that he would be free to break off his engagement as an aircraftman second class whenever he so chose, and without notice. Furthermore, thanks to the preparations he had made before enlisting, he believed that he could count upon the protective intervention of powerful friends. He set off for the void, but he did not fail to leave a forwarding address:

'In case I'm wanted by the Colonial Office, I'll send you a note as often as I change stations,' he wrote to Air Vice-Marshal Sir Oliver Swann two days after his arrival at Uxbridge; his despair is visible in this letter: 'I leap into the air when I am spoken to unexpectedly, and can't reply a word: only stand there shivering. And it's hard not to give oneself away at such moments.'

He sent copies of *The Seven Pillars of Wisdom* to several writers, among whom was Bernard Shaw. In a long letter accompanying the book, he wrote to Shaw: 'If you say it is all possible, then I will reluctantly get rid of your own books from my shelves.' He wrote to Edward Garnett: 'If your opinion (is) favourable, it would be wasted on me.'

He was by then at the training camp. Each day brought its new load of humiliations, notably on the part of a sergeant who had a ferocious dislike for him and treated him as a 'feeble imbecile', attacks which his victim did not succeed in standing up to. His body was constantly threatened with collapse, and weariness tortured him like an illness. His utter misery is easily recognised in the notes that he wrote each evening. (They were later to be published with the title of *The Mint*.) This particular practical joke threatened to end very badly indeed. More than ever he needed encouragement and admiration. With trembling hands he reached for the letters from outside that would tell him that he was indeed the author of a great book, but he continued to play a part in the comedy of his own creation—to play it before himself, and himself alone, as well as in his letters: bad cess to those who might find the courage to admire his book!

When the first comments reached him, and were enthusiastic, he began to live again. 'It's very good of you to praise my book so, and makes me very proud. I lap it up with both hands—the praise that is—the more greedily that it is the first judgment I have had,' he wrote to Edward Garnett. And he asked for more. To obtain it, he insisted upon his own discontent, maintaining that what he had wished to do was to add one more to the three 'titanic' books (*War and Peace, Zarathustra* and *Moby Dick*) this fourth book to be in English: his own.

Shaw took rather a long time reading the book, and had to be jogged along more than once. When at last he gave his opinion, Lawrence replied in those doubtful phrases that authors employ when they wish to extract yet further compliments from a benevolent critic. He made use of all the tricks, clearly unaware of how often they had been used by others, and of how many writers had stooped to this—and not only the authors of first books. For the first time he found himself involved in that very ancient comedy which so many others had played before him. But still he imparted to it a certain originality: never, he announced, would he publish his book. Or at least he would go no further than to permit the printing of extracts. (These were to appear with the title, *Revolt in the Desert*.) Or if he were to publish it in its entirety, it would be in a very expensive edition and an extremely limited one. For in literature, too, he practised that technique of secrecy which attracts interest more effectively than any other: similarly at the recruiting office he had behaved so strangely that senior officers had to intervene twice in order to silence the suspicions that he had aroused. When disappearing into the void, he took with him the royal brevet, a roll of parchment on which he was nominated British Representative in Trans-jordania. When, a few months later, a scandal temporarily ended his service with the R.A.F., Sir Oliver Swann could say that the true identity of John Hume Ross had been made public thanks to the imprudence of the Colonial Office and to 'Lawrence's unfortunate love of drawing a veil of mystery about himself.'

Using another name—T. E. Shaw—he enlisted in the Tank Corps, from which he was later transferred once again to the R.A.F. and sent on garrison duty near Karachi and finally to a post on the Afghan Frontier. Meanwhile *Revolt in the Desert* had appeared, as well as a limited edition of *The Seven Pillars of Wisdom*. Their enormous success affected him profoundly. He read the reviews attentively and reacted as all intelligent authors do: praise made him more modest, sometimes even sincerely humble. He was at last capable of expressing the happiness that he felt when someone, no matter who, spoke well of his work.

He read to Edward Garnett and other writers, including E. M. Forster, the notes which he was later to work up into *The Mint,* and once again became involved in his usual complicated strata-gems. Finally he decided that this book must not be published before 1950. The reasons that he gave for this seem as uncon-vincing to us as does the enthusiasm shown for this book by its first readers.

Early in 1929 Lawrence was recalled to England because newspapers throughout the entire world had published 'infor-mation' according to which this 'spy of genius' had stirred up the rebellion which lost Amanullah his throne in Afghanistan. Back in London, he had no trouble in persuading certain Labour M.P.'s, anxious to ask questions in the House concerning these alarming rumours, that he was not a master spy in the pay of the Intelligence Service, but the victim of his own legend. He was allowed to remain in the R.A.F., but henceforth he was surrounded by technicians and officers, all of whom knew that T. E. Shaw was Lawrence of Arabia. He was given reasonable work to do, and allowed to do it in conditions more suitable to a man of his status.

Slowly he learned how not to be unhappy, how to be reconciled with his being and to dispense with his 'fiction'. This is clearly revealed in a letter which he wrote on 4th February, 1935, to Robert Graves, one of his 'official' biographers, and a man who for some considerable time was the privileged recipient of those myths with which Lawrence embellished his existence: 'Don't give too much importance to what I did in Arabia during the war,' he wrote. He declared that the conquest of the air was the greatest task of his generation and added: 'I have convinced myself that progress today is not made by the single genius, but by the common effort.'

His period of enlistment being over, he left the R.A.F. in February of 1935. This was not the return of Haroun-al-Rashid. His life had become normal, his little house, Clouds Hill, had long been waiting ready, with his furniture, his books and his gramophone records. Waiting too, at least in the beginning, were the journalists from London. This time Lawrence really did not desire publicity. He fled from them, and only returned after some time had elapsed. The fear of living, for which he had so often found over-compensation in flight, never truly left him, nor the apprehension of an empty future; but he no longer systematically opposed his private logic to the logic of human existence.

Returning home on his motorcycle on May 13th, 1935, Lawrence was in a serious accident. He lingered in a coma for five days before he died.

Of all his passions, his passion for speed was the one that endured the longest. It was the only one, too, which can have flattered his ill-loved and finally subjugated body. And it was this passion that killed him.

3

In the spring of 1936 Lawrence's bust was unveiled in the crypt of St Paul's Cathedral. This ceremony added the official stamp of approval to a legend which was to go on growing. Not only did Imperial Britain seem to need this legend; it was acceptable, and indeed longed for throughout the whole world by intellectuals in search of a hero-thinker and of a metaphysics of action which they thought to find consecrated in the author of *The Seven Pillars of Wisdom*, the typical and exemplary man of the century: the lay saint, the philosopher-adventurer, the monk without a faith, and, in addition to that, apparently the liberator of twenty, forty or even sixty million Arabs. He was indeed a layman, occasionally an adventurer, without faith, but there was nothing of the liberator about him. He remains the author of *The Seven Pillars of Wisdom;* he will retain a fame that is justified by a book and not by a legend.

As a psychological case Lawrence is no more interesting than are so many persons with neuroses caused by a puritanism from which they have failed to escape, or of which they have repented ill; and such cases are encountered with great frequency in Protestant countries, particularly Anglo-Saxon ones. The extremity of his attitudes is in no way astonishing to the psychologist. Those attitudes complicated his life, but make the explanation of certain of his choices all the easier.

André Malraux, in no wise the dupe of Lawrence's 'fiction' nor of his legend, considers his adventure in Arabia as well as his flight towards humiliation as phases in a constant pursuit of the absolute. Those French writers who have taken up this theme, usually, it may be added, exaggerating both its terms and its dimensions, have not known how to protect themselves from the myths, and have ridiculously inflated their hero under the pretence of analysing him.

This need of the absolute can be easily explained, not only in the case of a man who, according to Malraux's view of Lawrence, was, 'one of the most religious spirits of his time, if by the religious spirit is understood that which feels, to the very bottom of its

soul, the anguish of being a man.' For each one of us, at every
period of his life, encounters this anguish; and a more or less
conscious need of the absolute is as widespread as the fear of no
longer existing. The means for deliverance from the one as from
the other are more or less identical. What made Lawrence's case
tragic was his inability to search for the absolute (which he lacked
the strength to renounce) in either a faith or a cause. He sought it
in himself: in his actions, which he magnified to grotesque
proportions.

Spiritually incapable of forging a link with other beings or
with causes, Lawrence, in his search for the certainty of his own
value, tried to define himself in relationship with his actions, to
justify through them an existence which he desired to be
absolutely independent, and to find in them his grandeur. Now
actions once accomplished have departed from us forever, and
their consequences create an infinite distance between us and them.
They may be regretted like lost youth, but they cannot be made
to live again. Lawrence remained the *veuf inconsolable,* the
widower whom none can console, mourning his revolt in the
desert.

A social upheaval, the war, gave to Lawrence as a young man
the unexpected possibility of acting at a level of efficiency which,
without the war, would doubtless have been denied to Hogarth's
assistant. This same accident offered bank clerks, lawyers, poets
and many others the possibility of transforming themselves into
leaders of men beneath a storm of fire and steel. Some of these
were to preserve a nostalgic memory, and to try for long years
to share this with all the world, in an attempt to ensure the
survival of these strange moments from their past. But most knew
that the greatness of their actions did not really belong to them.
As time went by they became more and more aware of the
irreducible disproportion between their own size and the immeasurable size evident in the results of the actions in which they
had been engaged. The man whose finger presses the button that
sends a hydrogen bomb against an enemy city would fall prey to
an annihilating folly if he lost sight of this disproportion, if he
failed to perform that act of separation which permits a man not

to integrate himself with his own actions. The leader of the attack on the Winter Palace, the intellectual Antonoff-Ovsëenko, knew that he was nothing more than a *delegate*. Only a megalomaniac would have thought that what the revolutionaries were doing was being done solely on his own initiative: that he was the Russian Revolution. Both Lenin and Trotsky knew that they were nothing more than the representatives of definite social forces already existing, the delegates of an historic movement.

As Lawrence became more and more aware of the truth—namely that this revolt in the desert did not in fact exist on the sublime plane where first he had placed it—the more it became his own private revolt: a strictly personal business. This identification had nothing to do with any metaphysics, with the satisfaction of any need for the absolute, but was concerned with the amazement of a young intellectual at the discovery of his own power and his own efficiency when mixed up in the affairs of others: the others in this case being military specialists of limited intellect, politicians lost in a routine, leaders discouraged by past failure. It is the wonderment of a Saint-Just, sent to reorganize the armies; but that young revolutionary adhered to a cause, while Lawrence sought to find the motives for his actions only in his intimate 'fiction'. He found them there at the cost of mystifying both himself and others. He might perhaps have regained his true road in 1919, had he not by then become possessed of a thunderous glory, which compelled him to incarnate his triumph and to perpetuate himself at the summit of his greatest warrior-hours. An official post, even a very high one, would have put him into an established hierarchy, in a career. Now in the desert he had felt himself to be above every hierarchy; he succeeded in remaining outside. A reader will have misunderstood *The Mint* badly if he has failed to recognise in it the image of a god humiliated and crucified by his own wish. This motif recurs with psychotics, notably in that terrifying depression, which, in the case of melancholics, alternates with a maniacal exaltation.

No, I certainly can find no metaphysical teaching in Lawrence, apart from that which each of us gives in the interpretation of a destiny that is treated individually.

There remains the confusing, purely historical phenomenon of his legend.

There is what might be described as a subterranean relationship between the glory of Napoleon and that of Victor Hugo. Hugo's glory is a reply to Napoleon's: it is a proud repentance. It was obviously essential that the poet, too, assume the rôle of a man of action, that he too become a source of national energy. But, even more, it was absolutely imperative that, face to face with the man of power, he should incarnate the man of spirit who must suffer before he may triumph. (Châteaubriand had foreseen exactly such a rôle for himself, and his *Mémoires d'outre-tombe* were designed to secure it for him. But they simply succeeded in destroying a few legends, and in creating none . . .)

Who dare affirm that, after the Great War, humanity was ashamed of herself, of her military enthusiasm, of her murderous hatred? The fact is that humanity tried to forget all that, even more quickly than the wooden crosses were rotting in the military cemeteries. Humanity sought, instead, for glories essentially different from those of the war. One symptom of this was the fact that all over the world newspaper readers displayed a most extraordinary enthusiasm for the three least heroic figures possible to imagine: Charlie Chaplin, Einstein, Freud. No explanation is necessary for Chaplin's legend; it was available to all the world. But how about Einstein? Men were willing, and indeed anxious, to believe that his theory was of tremendous importance, but they could not understand it. This peaceful and apparently inefficient little man was an ideal figure to help humanity forget the field marshals. Sigmund Freud's theory was scarcely understood any better, but it was felt that his discoveries offered additional reasons for not attaching too much belief to the words of infallible authorities.

The immense respect enjoyed at that time by those two scholars differed in quality to that given to a man such as Edison; it differed precisely in that few people could perceive anything useful in their work. The fact that they had triumphed without bloodshed and without recourse to power confirmed the newspaper readers in their open-mouthed admiration, which in fact was an unconscious and proud form of repentance.

There are in truth two Lawrence legends: in the first he is a Napoleon, in the second a Byronic Victor Hugo. If Aldington had contented himself with attacking the first legend, that of the triumphant warrior as portrayed by the American, Lowell Thomas, a purely British legend, he might have succeeded in weakening it considerably. The other, the legend of repentance, would have ceased to exist long ago if *The Seven Pillars of Wisdom* were as bad a book as Aldington claims it to be. And it would have disappeared of its own long since, if Lawrence, instead of becoming an aircraftman second class, had agreed to embark upon a career in the Colonial Office or had accepted the position of High Commissioner of Egypt. Public enthusiasm would soon have waned, and his successes in private life would have placed him on an equal footing with many other men of his generation. Heroism had first to become ironical, then repentant, then self-denying and finally self-humiliating before becoming (with the help of a vast publicity) esoteric, in order to seduce so many intellectuals to a point at which they confounded a partly-lived 'fiction' with a metaphysic incarnate.

It is true that this confusion characterises the situation, the false situation, of many intellectuals of our age. Action attracts them, though they scarcely participate in it; or they abandon their rôle of intellectuals by transforming their cause into a myth. They have learned that the act is not the man, but they go on believing in the existence of permanent heroes. They would 'transcend' all social facts, but they abstain from learning what those facts are in the first place.

It is their false situation which encourages the second Lawrence legend, itself the product of a false situation. The intellectuals will abandon it when they no longer feel a need for mystifications flattering to themselves.

July 1955

THE PUBLIC AND ITS SOUL

The Public and its Soul

It scarcely matters whether aesthetics are 'a law of the senses' rather than a logic of beauty, a theory of taste rather than a grammar of art, if they should be considered as a propaedeutic discipline or as a 'science of the spirit' (*Geisteswissenschaft*) and so on and so forth. The history of aesthetics is easy enough to follow, being contained in a philosophy that originated about the Mediterranean and later spread through all Europe. Refused existence by Plato, formulated by Aristotle, established by the Hellenists, rejected by the Christian thinkers, rediscovered by those of the Renaissance, baptised with its actual name by a Leibnitzian, defined by Vico as a poetic logic (in distinction to intellectual logic), it was finally put in its proper place by Kant in his *Critique of Judgment,* and systematised, needless to say, by Hegel.

Since the beginning of the last century aesthetics have developed in every direction: no man would dare boast that he knew so much as the titles of all the works devoted to this subject.

Works on aesthetics are usually divided into three main categories: theories, encyclopaedias and monographs. But analytically this immense literature can more truly be divided into three fundamentally different concepts of aesthetics: the first deals with the artist: the second with what he creates considered as a privileged universe, or, so to speak, a second *natura naturans:* the third is a concept of functional or social aesthetics. There are finally two tendencies which are juxtaposed when they are not opposed: the one would define art and its content in terms of interchanging forms: the other would search in the content and its open or hidden meanings for the law which governs all change of form.

No aesthetic research can avoid the question of value, a question asked by every work of art as insistently as every form of life demands the reason for its being. Traditional aesthetics, conceiving of absolute values, proposed to establish absolute and

eternal criteria. People are more modest today. The psychologist
studying the creator, the philosopher studying his creation, and
the historian studying civilisations, all tend to accept a scale of
values which sees greatness only in relativity. Certain works of
art suggest a new criteria, and outlive them; others, conforming
to established criteria, die with them. Any work of art which,
sooner or later, cannot succeed in educating its own public and
creating a sensitivity which sees itself reflected in that work, must
necessarily be of an ephemeral nature.

The commercial value of an artistic production is determined
by the intensity and the endurance of the satisfaction that it gives
to a need which must be sufficiently widespread. The relationship
between supply and demand thus controls the market in those
curious merchandises which are pictures, books, songs and so on.
Yet a work of art is very often without any 'exchange value'
because it does not encounter any demand until it has itself
provoked that demand: it is only desired after it has been found,
which is sometimes a very long time indeed after the artist himself
has disappeared.

Now a value which is not recognised or not known is a social
absurdity, comparable to a wind that does not blow. Even solitude means nothing apart from social relations: the solitude of a
hermit makes sense in so far as it is a withdrawal from the
organised communities which he is abandoning. In the domain of
what is called practical life, usage furnishes the criteria needed
for evaluation; but, in ethics as in aesthetics, values, even when
they are born of solitude, are a social phenomenon. When
unrecognised they remain a secret of which no man suspects the
existence. During an epoch when art represents society as it would
appear, thus lending to the myths of grandeur or of piety the
appearance of reality, an accursed artist (*l'artiste maudit*) is
unthinkable. Art becomes a curse when it is separated from its
society, opposed to it and intent solely on expressing its own
greatness: when it chooses no longer to be a means towards an
end, and decides to be its own end.

Now in the very beginning art produced those means which a
community uses in order to affirm its group communion in its

relations with those magical forces which have to be conciliated or
seduced; the means necessary to arouse collective enthusiasm and
to affirm courage when confronted by danger; to bear witness of
loyalty towards the past; to glorify the government of the elders;
to invent the secrets of the mysteries; and, finally, to protect
tabus. Art came before the artist, of whom no originality was
demanded—it would indeed have been sacrilege—but only an
absolute fidelity in the expression of meanings which had already
been precisely defined. The cult mask, the steps of a ritual dance,
the words of incantations, war songs and hunting songs, none of
these needed to be beautiful, but simply effective, that is to say
they must correspond without the slightest variation to forms
passed down by oral tradition.

It will easily be understood that an illiterate society should be
particularly rigid in its conception of forms: its consciousness is
nourished by the memory of the elders, who maintain their
importance by ensuring that the present shall exactly resemble the
past of which they alone preserve the recollection. In those
primitive societies where the elders rule, all forms are dogmatised,
and each is transformed into a symbol; just so are rites dogmatised
when religion is transformed into a triumphant church. The
symbol, a condensed content, consumes, so to speak, its form; this
form is nothing in itself, but it is sanctified by the sacred nature of
that which it will more often recall or insinuate than express. Thus
primitive men regard their works of art in the same way that the
modern interpreter of dreams regards a dream: he knows that
each of the elements composing the dream-story is nothing in
itself, but that it indicates the presence of a condensed content
which the dreamer's associations will perhaps reveal.

The transition from the sorcerer-elder to the artisan-artist
doubtless occurs as a result of the division of labour, inevitable
when a certain level of production has been reached, and as the
result of wars and invasions which lead to the confrontation of
dogmatised forms that seem mutually exclusive and that yet must
be reconciled.

When victorious invaders did not exterminate the natives, they
imposed their laws upon them, but they had to allow their forms

to become intermingled with those of the vanquished. In these conditions it was the task of the artisan-artist to combine these frequently contradictory elements and to 'syncretise' rival forms and conflicting myths. In order to cause a new formal unity to arise from the original diversity, the artist obtained a doubtless tacit freedom of creation, but not the right to claim this; he might not present himself as the author of the message, but merely as the man who had carried out orders received from above.

It is easier now than it was two thousand years ago to discern this work of syncretisation and of editing which created the Pentateuch and the songs of Homer, and we can distinguish the conquering gods which are there being united, the myths of diverse origins which are being reconciled. But we shall never know who first sang the song of Deborah, and we shall probably be unaware forever as to the true part that Homer (or that the two Homers) played in the creation of the epics that are immortalised under this name.

Even in a period far closer to our own, in a civilisation superbly mature—the height of the fifth century at Athens—a work such as the Parthenon Athene was doubtless in the first place a divine object, and only the highly educated minority can have regarded it as the creation of an artist. We do know of the very serious trouble in which Phidias found himself as the result of his attempt to put himself into his work: he was not forgiven for having carved his own effigy and that of Pericles upon the shield of the goddess. Similarly, it is most unlikely that when confronted by the cathedrals of the Middle Ages, or later by the frescoes in the churches, the faithful should have stopped for one moment to ask aesthetic questions, or should have felt the slightest wish to know the name of the men whose works stoked the ardour of their faith. The faithful did not attempt to judge a representational work, but to forget that it was a representation, for they wished to see in it the very beings that they worshipped. They sought neither art nor beauty, but divine efficacy.

For thousands of years the true nature of the plastic arts was public, that is to say social or religious, though this certainly does not explain either the genius of Phidias nor the absence of artistic

genius of Socrates who, at the same period, was helping his father
to produce those remarkable precursors of Victorian religious art
which lined the road to the Piraeus. Nor can social aesthetics
explain the genius of Aeschylus and Sophocles, when they set
about transforming into tragedies stories already known to all
the world. But the social conditions which compelled Phidias to
eliminate his own personality from his works, so that once they
had left his hands they might become sacred, were the same which
determined the choice of content and form of the Athenian
tragedies. (It is possible that the Athenians also wrote plays which
did not conform. This certainly must have been the case with
Euripides.)

Until comparatively recent times literature remained for
everyone, save the author himself and a very small élite, a
phenomenon of sound. People listened, they did not read. Just
one century ago the percentage of illiterates in Great Britain
amounted to 32 per cent among men and 48.9 per cent among
women. It is reckoned that nowadays 40 per cent of the population of the world (aged ten or more) know how to read and
write. This estimate might prove optimistic if the reader were
asked to do more than simply identify the letters and painfully
reconstruct the word that they compose. Reading a book still
constitutes an unusual effort for the majority of those who,
statistically speaking, are not illiterate. The troubadour and the
professional story-teller have not been replaced by books, but by
the talkies, the radio, television and newspapers. The written word
is less attractive than images (comic strips and illustrations) and
than spoken words which reach even those who refuse to make
any effort whatsoever. After all, a musician writes his notes for
specialists, and his music does not exist for the public until it is
played by those specialists, that is to say transformed into sound.
Literature, the art of words, is first of all song, the composition of
groups of rythmic words, and later a theatrical spectacle. It is an
art, which, for the great public, exists only in public. The solitary
reader, alone with the intimacy of a book, remained for a very
long time a member of a small and privileged social group.

Homer sang for his public and Sophocles wrote for it. But what about Thucydides? We know *why* that exile became the historian of a war in which he had taken part as a military leader on the side of his compatriots, before observing it from the point of view of the man rejected into no-man's land and cast among his people's enemies. But *for whom* did he write it? Surely for those who in any event could never hear his voice, for they were not yet born. Death, probably violent death, prevented him from carrying his extraordinary undertaking to its end. But for that he might perhaps have revealed to us more clearly which of the lessons he intended to bequeath to the future would contain his justification. Since he was addressing that future, his text differs from what his contemporaries were writing: he did not intend his words to be spoken, but to be seen, read. It is in this sense that he is the first real modern writer: a lonely man, speaking to another, unknown to him, and who does not yet exist.

An author writing for unknown readers is a new phenomenon, which has become a common one since the invention of printing. Like a sculptor or a painter who knew in advance where his work was destined to go, a writer in the old days knew whom he was addressing. That is why rhetoric remained inevitable until the time when the anonymous reader began to replace the listening audience; when the writer began writing for a man who must have solitude in order to catch the author's meaning.

'For everyone and for no one.' Nietzsche's dedication characterises well enough the simultaneous existence of two contradictory tendencies: when an artist does not create for a designated public which he knows and whose tastes or needs he desires to satisfy, then he conceives of a universal, but non-existent, public. Thus the artist works for himself and for himself alone. In our times the most subjective abstract art that exists is made to be hung in exhibitions; it is addressed to all the world and to nobody in particular, like posters stuck up in the streets.

It seems that Cervantes used to tell his tales about Don Quixote to his fellow prisoners in order to earn his daily soup. When later he published his novel, he knew who his readers would be and to what extent they were prepared to receive his gigantic pastiche. If Rembrandt quarrelled with the burghers of Amsterdam, whom he portrayed in his *Night Watch*, he nevertheless regarded them for a long time as his public, that is to say his patrons. Lesage wrote down stories which were being told everywhere, and people read him in order to have stories to tell. It was at this time that prose fiction began to replace those magical and hagiographical tales of the Jack-and-the-Beanstalk variety, transforming the hero, without relieving him of his archetypal attributes nor delivering him from the yoke of destiny. This sort of fiction, as popular today as when first it was created, has changed with the times: it recounts the same conflicts, but adapts them to the experience of contemporaries and tells them in terms of the present. As the result of some personal, family or general misfortune, or due to his own blindness, the hero is taken out of his environment, thrown into the unknown, and delivered to a world which is now indifferent, now hostile. Whether he wishes it or not, his life is henceforth nothing but a series of adventures, unexpected discoveries, terrifying or lucky encounters, good or bad fortune. The exaggerated anguishes and hopes which inspired the tales of folklore are resurrected in modern fiction, and are received with gratitude and affection by a public that has been immensely enlarged owing to the cinema. This literature has the realism of dreams; it insinuates itself painlessly into the unconscious of spectator and reader alike, by flattering his nostalgias and his most secret desires. Novelty of form maintains the public's interest, but in order not to risk deceiving that public it is necessary that, beneath these new forms, the same substance should reappear each time. Only secondary variations are wanted: the orphaned boy is now changed into an orphaned girl, who is made to live in a more picturesque period of history, and the heroines always emerge unscathed from their photogenic cataclysms, thanks to their victorious beauty and to their remarkable skill in subterfuge.

The reader of this sort of literature expects that it will allow him to enter into an extraordinary world while simultaneously and at all times guaranteeing to him that that world is in fact authentic: it must regale him with stories which are not stories, but the truth, something which really happened. The writer poses not as the author of his tales, but as the agent who transmits them. He frequently maintains in asides, if not in the very form that he gives to his story, that his imagination is never at any time responsible for what he writes—imagination means lies. The reader usually does not notice the name of the author, or forgets it very rapidly, but he will remember the title of the book a little longer. He will ask his library or his book-seller for 'another one of the same sort'. Thus the people who go to the movies do not know the name of the producer or of the director: their choice is decided by a desire to see 'another film of the same sort' and to find again their favourite actors and actresses constantly reincarnating the same personages in the same situations. They need no fresh effort in order to identify themselves with the hero, and indeed after the second or third film identification is established the moment the film begins. In this a visit to the cinema resembles a conditioned reflex.

Neomania, that is to say the thirst for novelty, seems to be the one characteristic that all publics have in common: the readers of gossip columns as much as the audiences at cinemas. This may be regarded as the expression of a natural curiosity which, like hunger, is periodically revived and demands fresh satisfaction. Fresh but not new, for these neomaniacs always reveal a terror of novelty as soon as they are confronted with the unknown. They will scarcely tolerate the unknown save perhaps in the form of tiny surprises offered them by some new methods of presentation, but never in so far as the main content is concerned. The story of a crime, of a love first crossed but finally conquering, of some extraordinary exploit in the midst of mortal danger, fascinating circus turns, sweet melodies—all that only exerts an irresistible attraction when it is poured into moulds to which they are accustomed. They will, so to speak, only eat predigested food. For centuries it was compulsory that the principle figures in farces designed to make such a public laugh should always have the same names: a change of name or of costume threatened to annoy them as much as it worried them, the unaccustomed rousing in them a feeling of frustration. The great comic authors, in order to smuggle their originality across, had to keep to the sets and the typical protagonists of traditional farce.

Boccaccio, Cervantes, Swift, Defoe, Dickens and Mark Twain are the great authors of modern times whose masterpieces still influence a vast public throughout the entire world. They created prototypes which are recreated each year in countless versions. The authors of these versions are presumably in most cases unaware that they are copyists, for what they write corresponds only too often to their own dreams (and at the same time—by a lucky coincidence—to the demands of the market). Neither the industrial revolution, nor political upheavals, nor two world wars have sufficed to change the public's tastes—or its dreams. The prototypes crystallised, and the destinies revealed, in the work of those great writers continue to fascinate a public which itself is Sancho Panza; knowing everything about Don Quixote, he yet never hesitates to set off with the Knight Errant towards new adventures which remain always and essentially the same.

Zola, Gorki and Upton Sinclair detached a part of this popular public from its dreams and immunised it against the charms of evasion. The proletarian heroes of their novels were not heroes in isolation, nor converted Don Quixotes, nor seduced Sancho Panzas, but beings representative of a mass formed of and by their equals. *Germinal, The Mother* and *Jimmie Higgins*, are type-books in which the reader, more fond of fiction than of literature, sought for awareness, the reasons for his social being, and the courage to continue the struggle in an exalting solidarity.

In them he found 'real life', his own misfortunes, ordinary social facts, and not extraordinary individual adventures; he found, in fact, himself as reflected to him by his own experiences.

This sort of fiction was a development of the reporter's craft, and established itself as historical novels cast in the present. It conditioned the manner of seeing and thinking for countless readers; for half a century it had a political effect far deeper than that of doctrinaire writing or of propaganda. Furthermore, it decided the character of most of the war stories written after 1918 and influenced the development of those prose writers, in Russia and elsewhere, between 1919 and 1934, who dealt with the theme of a revolutionary *Pilgrim's Progress*.

All this seemed to promise a great future. It came to nothing.

Soviet literature was systematically ruined by the servitude imposed upon it in the name of a false aesthetic called 'socialist realism', and everywhere else in the world Communist literature followed its example. At the same time popular taste seems to have veered away from proletarian reading. The public that came into existence at the beginning of the century had few successors; stories and films designed to satisfy a dream-need once again won the day.

In the middle of our century, the heroes of fiction are master criminals, highly skilled detectives, the knowledgeable technicians of science fiction, and, even more than all of them, women and the girl orphans carried away in the storms of past dramas. It may be noted that those champions of the football or other sporting fields, whose activities, both professional and private, seem to enthrall the masses when they are recounted as a daily and newspaper-fabricated myth, lose all their *charisma* as soon as they are subjected to a literary or cinematographic transposition. And despite the adoration that this century has hitherto granted to its 'men of destiny'—Hitler, Mussolini, Stalin—these idols exercise no enduring attraction when transposed into fiction. In these years of global war and of world-wide victories, the public becomes more and more certain that the dreams of triumph only makes sense when applied to the destinies of women: Theodora, Catherine, Scarlett, Amber, Caroline, Désirée, and all the rest of them. The goddesses of the past, with their striking resemblance to the mediocre stars of technicolour cinema, are steadily and invincibly making their way back up into the empty skies.

This is by no means a question of that phenomenon which Malraux has defined as a 'metamorphosis', a dialectical phenomenon whereby the perennial nature of art is affirmed. Social aesthetics, observing the arts from the point of view of the consumer and not of the creator, reveal that during the thousands of years in which we know of men's taste, that taste may have changed from time to time, but only in terms of what is, in the narrowest sense, its form of expression, its jargon, and never at all in terms of its content.

It would certainly be an error to under-estimate the importance of such a change and to ignore its relationship with social transformations, whether infra- or supra-structural, to use Marx's words. Differences undoubtedly exist between a Roman Catholic novel designed to prove the truth of that faith and a Communist novel with equally good intentions: the selective principles employed by the sincere falsifiers of reality are philosophically opposed. The reader of the one as of the other—his mental age is not twelve, but thirteen—there finds evil personified: the sinner (sacrilege) or the counter-revolutionary (saboteur or lascivious viper); and there also displayed for his admiration is goodness transformed into man: the virtuous, practising believer on the one hand, the devoted revolutionary member of the Party on the other. The content of this sort of fiction is the Manichaean duel, and although the public knows in advance what the result of the struggle will be, it awaits it each time with anxiety in order to rejoice afresh and to be able to fortify its faith. (It is only necessary to recall the repetitive dream which accompanies the years of youth: there too the stereotyped scenario in no way diminishes the tension of waiting.)

In modern detective stories and tales of high adventure, moral Manichaeism seems to be somewhat weaker, the goodness of the good characters and the victory of virtue less of a foregone conclusion than they used to be. The reader nowadays is prepared to allow innocent characters in extreme situations to make use of those ruses and subterfuges which used to belong exclusively to the wicked. The wicked remain a constant threat, and yet the reader prefers to see innocence persecuting rather than persecuted. It is given full permission to act according to the rules of 'anticipated legitimate self-defence'. That our contemporary public should allow virtue the right to be as violent and as brutal as evil cannot solely be explained by the propaganda which, during the wars, glorified murder; there is also a secondary explanation in a growing impatience with the slow development of epic tales. The influence of the cinema and of television is probably greater in this than is that of the newspapers and of sound radio: sixty or at the most one hundred minutes suffice to make the spectator the direct witness of a drama which is unrolled with an extreme rapidity and in which the end and the climax very frequently coincide. A public educated in the cinemas is less and less willing to endure an epic tale, and is hardly ready to forgive that *anticlimax* which no true novel ever succeeds in avoiding entirely. It is thanks to its especial violence, a continual explosion of an exaggeratedly condensed time, that cinematographic fiction agrees better than any other presentation of an imagined reality with the essence of dreams. In films humanity encounters at last what it has always been looking for in its legends, its myths, its epics, in its theatre and in its traditional heroic tales: the possibility of taking part in the life of others by identifying oneself with those others, of experiencing adventures and suffering but at secondhand, and finally of surviving death. The magic of speaking pictures shows that the public was right to demand of true fiction that it be the fiction-of-truth: that it present the past ('stories') not as a memory but as an incarnation of the present. The sex-appeal of the star playing Cleopatra seduces the spectator and thus convinces him that this queen of Egypt really existed and really seduced great men. Real fiction only succeeds in 'deceiving', whereas the fiction-of-truth begins by a seduction. And of all victims, only the victims of seduction feel that they have won a victory.

It is being said everywhere that literature is dying, and that the novel is already dead. This is not at all the case. Undoubtedly a certain type of fiction is losing its public, because that public no longer reads it but swallows it in the form of a filmed dramatisation. So what is happening is a displacement and not a disappearance. Common consumption, a social phenomenon of great importance, is once again becoming the normal way in which the populace absorbs fictions. (Television is not reversing this evolution, but adding a variant to it: even spatial separation does not prevent this public consumption. An identical invitation, at the identical hour, is offered to all.) One result of this is that a growing number of novels are written and published solely with a view to being transformed into films.

All this has nothing to do with literature. The readers of literature are, both relatively and absolutely, more numerous than

ever before. Its social function, however, remains as ill-defined as
has been that of the plastic arts for almost one hundred years.
The dramatic poems of Sophocles, of Shakespeare, of Racine and
of Schiller were addressed to a public which already existed; the
same applied to the comedies of Aristophanes, of Molière and of
Goldoni, as well as to the novels of Cervantes, Richardson,
Fielding, Jane Austen, Thackeray, Scott, Dickens, Balzac and
Dumas. On the other hand those of Benjamin Constant, of
Stendhal, of Dostoievsky, Joyce, Proust and Kafka were destined
for the solitary reader who, in fiction, did not look for adventures,
but for an encounter with consciousness; not for the dream, but
for the awakening.

This is a literature which uses fiction as the moralist uses fables
and the preacher parables. In the midst of a civilisation of gigantic
agglomerations and of masses organised into huge publics whose
taste is becoming increasingly imperious, this literature which
questions everything only affirms the solitude of man. Since it
usually serves neither a religion nor a cause, its pretensions must
be to be everything in itself: a religion without a god, a cause
without an end, thus an end in itself. This pretension is rarely
expressed and often contradicted (by Dostoievski among others),
but that in no way alters the alternatives: this literature, from
the point of view of social aesthetics, is either a lay gospel without
any message of hope, or nothing. The current vogue of
publishing diaries, collections of letters and monographs reveals
a tendency among artists to establish themselves as the unique
élite in a society whose hierarchy seems to have been shattered
forever. Let us imagine a Phidias returning to earth in order to
exact his revenge: he would deny or destroy his Parthenon
Athene, preserving only his self-portrait carved upon her shield.
A photograph of this, blown up to enormous proportions, would
show us the figure of a man who had known how to create gods.

Whether God be dead or not, the public—that is to say almost
all the world—needs gods for the care of its soul. The study of
these needs and of the care of souls is one of the first and most
important tasks of social aesthetics.

March 1955

Index